As missionaries  ne unspeakable loss of in a tragic snow-sledd[ing accident]... ul lessons she learned v... is flooded with works on how to deal with grief, but nothing I have ever read has affected me as has this volume. Each chapter draws from some aspect of her arduous journey of putting life back together. You will be indebted to her, not only for such helpful insights on grief, and how it can affect the suffering survivor, but also for her realistic advice to surviving victims struggling to make sense out of their misfortunes. While most sufferers are trying to discover why God has allowed their deep loss, Heather takes her reader into far more helpful ways to face life after grief. This volume should be an immediate read for anyone who is struggling to make sense of tragedy.

Paul L. Kaufman, Ph.D.
Seminary Professor, Chairman of Bible/Theology

The title of my message at Janette's funeral was "When Trouble Turns to Triumph." The tragedy was undeniable. But triumph? How could this horror turn to triumph for Ed and Heather Durham in those intensely dark days? It certainly was not in a sudden wiping away of the trauma. But it was in the miracle of "unexplained endurance" and unmoved faithfulness to their Heavenly Father. The book you hold in your hands is a testimony to the power of grace that triumphs in trouble. As you read, may our Father turn your trouble into triumph as He sustains you with "unexplained endurance" for your journey.

Rev. Blake Jones
Conference President
Great Lakes Bible Methodist Connection of Churches

In *An Unexplained Endurance*, Heather Durham offers deep insight and wisdom attained only by personally walking the arduous pathway of grief. She extends genuine hope and encouragement to fellow travelers weary from the journey. As I read, I found myself alternately crying, thanking God for His sustaining power, and saying aloud, "Wow, this will really help others who are grieving." This book contains the most poignant and beautifully written paragraph I have ever read. You will know which one it is when you read it.

Tom Sproles
Funeral Director, Sproles Family Funeral Home

Ed and Heather Durham have a lifetime of ministry experience that has been deeply enriched by 25 years of missionary service in Eastern Europe. As missionary educators in a communist country, they faced some of the most challenging circumstances one could ever imagine. However, nothing was to challenge their faith like the tragic death of their daughter. In *An Unexplained Endurance,* Heather opens for public view this dark chapter of their lives and shares what both grief and grace has taught them. As you walk with her on this seemingly endless journey of grief, you will be carefully led to each of God's signposts of encouragement and healing. This is a must read!

Dr. Michael Avery
Chancellor, God's Bible School and College

I highly recommend this excellent book by Heather Durham, because it helps us look at the limitations and disappointments of life through the lens of Jesus Christ. It is a great blend of honest, transparent reflection and practical, theological thinking. As soon as this riveting story is published, I will get it in the hands of everyone I know who is processing grief.

Dr. Dale R. Shillington
Associate Pastor, Church on the Rock

As a mother who has experienced the loss of a child, I can tell you that grief is a lifelong journey. Whether you have lost a child or someone else close to you, this book will help you navigate through your journey as Heather shares her story of grief and how to cope along the way. Everyone experiencing grief should read this book.

Jamie Rauschenberger
Gold Star Mother

This challenging book provides a window through which we watch as pain and loss intersect with healing and restoration. Heather's transparency and vulnerability is breathtaking as she invites us to walk with her through the dark valley of grief and into the light of grace. Her willingness to share her deepest doubts and fears helps us to understand the depths of God's love and care for His children. This quote says it well: "In our moment of greatest need, God's grace kept pace!"

Steve Stetler
Director of Missionary Member Care
Hope International Missions

An Unexplained Endurance is a heart wrenching story of a missionary couple's faith in the midst of great loss and pain. As you read this book, you will be confronted with the difficult realities of life and will learn that God is more than enough. This story will deepen your faith in God.

Dr. Mark A. Smith
President, Columbia University

I am deeply grateful to Heather for writing about her journey of grief. She relates her story in a transparent and candid way that speaks deeply into each of our lives. This book really touched my heart and I know it will be meaningful for each person who reads it, because we all experience loss and hardship at some time in our life.

Khalad Laci
Superintendent
Hungarian Methodist Church

In Loving Memory

Janette Joy Durham
September 3, 1984–February 16, 1996
~ *The girl who sang for Jesus* ~

An Unexplained Endurance

HOPE FOR THE JOURNEY OF GRIEF AND LOSS

HEATHER DURHAM

An Unexplained Endurance

Copyright 2021 by Heather Durham.
All rights reserved. No part of this book may be used or reproduced in any manner whatsoever without written permission except in the case of brief quotations embodied in critical articles or reviews.

ISBN 978-1-948362-59-7

Unless otherwise noted, scripture is taken from the New King James Version®. Copyright © 1982 by Thomas Nelson. Used by permission. All rights reserved.

Scripture marked NIV is from the Holy Bible, New International Version®, NIV® Copyright ©1973, 1978, 1984, 2011 by Biblica, Inc.® Used by permission. All rights reserved worldwide.

Cover design by Shane Muir

Published by Whispering Pines Publishers, Shoals, Indiana.

Printed in the United States of America.

CONTENTS

	Acknowledgments	9
	Foreword	11
	Introduction	13
1	Unwanted News	15
2	Darkness Settles In	21
3	Does God's Call Include This?	27
4	An Unexpected Harvest	33
5	Searching For Answers	39
6	In the Nick of Time	45
7	Finding My Way in the Dark	51
8	This Doesn't Change My Understanding of God	59
9	Surrounded by Prayers	65
10	It's Not a Sign of Weakness	71
11	Driving in the Fog	77
12	Choosing to Forgive	83
13	The Big Picture	89
14	Adjusting Our Expectations	95
15	Focus on the Positive	101
16	Everyone's Unique Journey	109
17	Broken to Serve	117
18	Does Time Heal?	123
	Endnotes	130

ACKNOWLEDGMENTS

My deepest and sincere thanks…

To my husband Ed, who supported me through each phase of this project and who allowed me to share some of his innermost thoughts and emotions with the world. Your strength is an inspiration to me.

To Alicia, who walked with us on this journey of grief and who cried with me as I put some of these heart-wrenching memories on paper. As a daughter and a friend, you are the best.

To each of our family, friends and missionary colleagues who loved and supported us during our time of heartbreak and grief. God used you to bring healing to our souls.

To Ezra Byer for guiding me from the beginning to the end of the process of writing this book. I deeply appreciate your encouragement and expertise.

To Beth Hawley, Gwen Wilson, Wesley Holden, Tom Sproles and Dr. Paul Kaufman for reading the manuscript and offering valuable feedback, suggestions for improvement and positive reinforcement. Your honest critiques were invaluable to me.

To my loving Heavenly Father whose grace is enough for every heartache and trial. I pray I have adequately conveyed your unfailing love and power through my story, so each reader will find comfort in your presence.

FOREWORD

In 1992, my husband Melvin and I felt compelled by God to sell everything we had, pack up our five children, our minimal clothing, and a few things we might need to move to Ukraine to start a Bible college and share the good news of the Gospel with the people there.

I was only twenty-eight years old, and my husband was thirty-two. I would be lying if I told you I didn't have some apprehension as we stepped off the plane in Kiev on that cool September day. We were excited, yet we already felt a sense of loneliness, since we had left our friends and family eight thousand miles behind in the United States. We settled in, started learning the language, and made friends, but with our broken Russian, communication wasn't always smooth. We longed to have someone with whom we could converse without an interpreter.

We learned that our mission board was sending Ed and Heather Durham and their two girls to help us in the college, and we were excited! Our kids were thrilled to have new friends to play with and even go to school with. I've lived long enough to understand that life brings good things and life brings bad things, but the news of the Durhams' arrival was a very good thing.

Our family and Ed and Heather's family hit it off from the start, and we became fast friends. I didn't teach in the college, so I would often watch their girls, Janette and Alicia, while Ed and Heather taught class in the evenings. Our oldest daughter and Janette became best friends, and many evenings, Erica and Janette would play school, insisting that all the other children participate. It was such a beautiful sound to hear the children playing together. Little did we know that the joy and laughter of the children's voices during our get togethers would be cut short by tragedy.

As I read through the chapters you are about to read, I relived the day that tragedy struck our missionary family. With tears streaming down my face, I was reminded that bad things come to each of us, and many times we can do nothing to prevent them. It seems unfair, and we have questions.

Maybe you're struggling with pain or grief or tragedy that you just don't understand. You see no answers and don't know where to turn. It has taken Heather twenty-five years to write the story of her grief journey. In these chapters, Heather has been honest in sharing the dark times and the happy times, but as you read through each chapter, I am confident you will find encouragement, healing, hope, and even some answers for the grief and pain you're experiencing.

So, grab a cup of coffee, find a cozy place to sit, and learn from someone who I have personally watched experience unspeakable pain, yet has come through it to write this book and encourage you.

—*Sandy Adams*

INTRODUCTION

As a teenager in middle school, I was a sprinter on the track and field team. At track meets, I won the hundred-yard dash almost every time because I was light, fast on my feet, and could push my body for quick energy. Longer races, however, were out of the question. My coach never slated me for one-mile races or long-distance runs because I had not learned to pace myself, nor had I built up the endurance necessary to win.

Later in life, when tragedy struck, I did not expect the journey of grief to be so long. I knew, of course, the first few months would be excruciating. However, with time, I expected to experience complete healing because that is what other people said would happen. I thought I would be back to my normal, pre-tragedy self in a few months. But my personal experience proved to be quite different.

The truth is, the journey of grief is unending, especially if the loss is sudden and traumatic. It requires emotional endurance that defies human explanation. The journey has hills and valleys and twists and turns; it takes you through both deep and shallow waters. It is not a sprint. It is a marathon. All of this begs one question: *Where do we find the endurance to survive and potentially thrive?*

Through my journey, I have discovered that God gives unexplained endurance as we navigate the uncharted pathways of grief. If we look for the beautiful flowers and listen for the whispers of God's sustaining grace along the way, we will find inner strength to walk the path God has chosen for us. If we cooperate with Him and maintain a strong faith in His perfect plan, we will be able to rest in His love for us. And, as we look back, we will see how His grace sustained us and transformed us into stronger yet more sensitive people.

My prayer for each of you, as you read this book, is that you will embrace your journey. God never promised we would sail smoothly through life with no grief, heartaches, valleys, or disappointments. My journey will not be identical to yours, but I pray that as I tell my story, you will be encouraged to find the faith to trust God for emotional strength and endurance for your journey. Lean hard on Jesus for grace and power to thrive amid pain and suffering.

I'm grateful that I can offer you this hope and assurance: God will give you the sustaining grace that you need.

1

UNWANTED NEWS

*It's not the moment that it happens,
It's the moment right before,
It's not the rain or crashing thunder,
It's the calm before the storm.*
—Kate Dudley

It was Friday, February 16, 1996. The girls bounced into the house after school, and the atmosphere exploded with their excitement. They scurried about like kittens chasing a ball of yarn, gathering their snow gear and preparing to rush back to sled on the hill beside the school. Their teacher, a wonderful young woman named Helen, had invited all the missionary girls for a sleepover at her home after they finished sledding. It promised to be a fun evening, complete with Valentine cookies and cupcakes.

As usual, our eleven-year-old daughter, Janette, was taking charge, making sure everyone was on task and no time was being wasted. She prodded her sister, Alicia, two years younger, to hurry, all the while continuing to chatter with her best friend, Erica. Using her natural charm, Janette asked her dad if he would drive them back to the school, about a mile away. Ed readily agreed, and they piled into our little red Lada for the quick trip to the school.

Our tiny house fell quiet again, and I went to the kitchen to finish preparing pumpkin for the freezer. With such a small workspace, pumpkin was everywhere. Still, the thought of making warm chocolate chip pumpkin bread and pumpkin pie for my family made the mess worthwhile. Since it was impossible to buy canned pumpkin in Ukraine, I enjoyed the satisfaction of having it in the freezer. In the coming months, it would be nice to bake a special treat for family and guests.

I looked at the clock and knew I needed to hurry. I was scheduled to teach a class that afternoon, and I wanted to get the pumpkin finished before it was time to leave. Ed would be back soon so I could take the car to class.

After finishing up the pumpkin, I wiped the countertop. The dishes could wait until later. I rushed to get ready. I collected my teaching materials, put them in my shoulder bag, and set it on a kitchen chair along with my purse and winter coat.

Where is Ed? What is he doing? He knew I needed to leave soon.

With no way to contact him, I sat at the table with a growing sense of impatience. We had no phone line in the house, and Ukraine had no cell phone service in those days either.

I tried to be calm, but the minutes kept ticking away. I imagined Ed flying into our driveway at the very last minute, so I put on my coat and boots and decided to walk out to the street to make each minute count. That way, I could hop in the car and take off the moment he arrived.

As I opened the door, the cold, crisp afternoon air hit me in the face, and snow flurries swirled around me. For the most part, I love winter. Growing up in Canada, I have wonderful memories of skating and tobogganing. There was always something special about the sun sparkling on the fresh snow and the invigorating feeling cold weather pumped into my body. But this winter had been long and dreary. The sun does not shine much in Kiev during the winter, so residents are left with endless days of overcast skies.

By February, it is common to hear people talk about "the grays"—and not just in reference to the weather. This term also describes the emotional depression that sets in because of the unending winter and lack of sun. My mother once visited us in Ukraine and remarked that, in ten days, she had only witnessed sunshine for two hours. While I had never kept track of the long gray days, we all knew it was a reality and that, subconsciously, the lack of sunshine took its toll on us.

Locking the door behind me, I walked down the sidewalk and out through the gate that enclosed our yard. The snow crunched under my feet as I stepped to the side of the road. No matter how many significant snowfalls we had during our long winter, the street in our little village on the edge of the city was never plowed, and the snow just continued to get packed down by cars. Sometimes the sun would be warm enough to melt some of the snow, but bright, sunny winter days were rare. This was one of those normal, snowy, overcast days.

I pulled the hood of my parka up over my head, fixed my scarf around my neck, and thrust my gloved hands into my coat pockets to keep them warm. Even though I was wearing my winter boots, my feet were getting cold standing in the snow, so I walked in place to try to keep them from freezing. I peered down the street to see if I could catch a glimpse of Ed approaching. Still, I saw no sign of him. *At least the girls are having fun*, I thought.

Again, I looked at my watch. Even if Ed arrived now, I would be late for class. *What is he doing? How inconsiderate can he be*? I became puzzled because this was so unlike him, and he knew how I hated to be late.

The sun sank lower in the afternoon sky, and dusk set in. Snow continued to fall, and the wind picked up a bit. When I couldn't stand in the cold any longer, I trudged back into the house, removed my coat, and sat at the kitchen table. *I'm not going to make it to class anyway,* I told myself as I stared out the window. All I could do was wait anxiously to catch the first glimpse of Ed as he walked up the sidewalk.

In my heart, I knew something had gone wrong. *Has he been stopped by the ever-present Ukrainian police? If he forgot his documents, it could be serious and take a long time to resolve. Has there been an emergency? Maybe someone without a car needed Ed to take them somewhere.* My mind raced, and I could not take my eyes off the window.

The minutes dragged by like hours. Then, through the dusk, I saw two people walking up the sidewalk to my door. It was our national leader, Valodia, and our missionary colleague, Twila. *How unusual! Why are Valodia and Twila coming to my door?* My heart beat faster.

I answered the door, my face filled with puzzlement and worry. They were subdued, serious. No smiles. No friendly greeting. Twila asked me to sit down. Then she spoke the words no one ever wants to hear. "There has been an accident," she said. I was numb. I stared at her. "Janette is gone, and Ed is in the hospital. He needs you. We need to go right away."

I was in a daze. Somehow, I put my coat and boots on and let Twila lead me to the car. We sat in the back seat as Valodia sped toward the hospital. The truth sank in, and I sobbed on Twila's shoulder. "No! No! Not Janette! Dear Lord, *please, please* help me!" The ache in my heart seemed unbearable.

The trip to the hospital was short, only ten minutes. Now the sun had set, and darkness settled its heavy blanket over the city. Like most of the buildings in Kiev, the hospital was a dreary cement building with only a couple of dim lights flickering beside the heavy wooden doors. As I got out of the car, I wondered what I would face inside that ominous building. Somehow, I knew I had to pull myself together. I had to be strong. Ed needed me. *What is wrong with him? Is he going to be okay?*

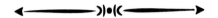

Reflecting on Your Journey

Can you identify the specific incident or time when you knew that you were being thrust onto the path of grief?

What emotions accompanied this moment in your life?

2

DARKNESS SETTLES IN

Be merciful to me, Lord, for I am in distress.
—Psalms 31:9, NIV

As we walked toward the doors of the hospital, the ever-growing darkness crept over me. It was like a black shroud had been thrown over my heart, twisting and tightening its grip on me. My mind became hazy, as if my brain had been depleted of oxygen. I experienced fear and dread like I had never known.

We passed through the heavy doors into a large, dim hallway with a single lightbulb dangling from the ceiling. The grungy cement floors with their messy pools of melted snow marked our way. Everything looked cold and grey. Here and there, a few straight wooden chairs lined the wall. People slouched in the chairs, clutching their drab woolen coats around their shoulders. Their faces were lined with weariness and boredom, tired of the long wait.

As we walked past them, I could feel their eyes following me. I wondered: *What do you see? Do you see my excruciating pain? Is it already etched in my face?* In my mind's eye, I was thinking of a sight I had seen so often, that of an old Ukrainian village woman trudging home from the forest with a heavy bundle of firewood strapped to her back. Beside her was her husband, carrying his axe. They were returning from the arduous task of cutting and gathering firewood to heat their modest home. *Now, I am like that old woman. Do you see this burden that has left me stooped over? It feels like a heavy bundle of firewood on my back. This burden is so great. How can I ever bear it?*

We entered a small room. The glare of light was startling in contrast to the dim hallway. Two small cots were pushed against opposite walls with a narrow space between them. Ed was laying on one cot. His face was pale and drawn. He didn't stir or look at me. Over the next few hours, I pieced together the events that had transpired after he left our home with a carful of excited girls.

It only took about five minutes for Ed to drive the girls from our home to the school. Janette and Erica bounded out of the car and ran toward the side of the building where the kids were sledding. The little hill sloped gently to a narrow street that ran in front of a large apartment building. A small snowbank at the bottom of the hill ran along the side of the road. Some Ukrainian kids had poured water on the hill so their sleds with metal runners would glide more easily and not get stuck in the new snow.

Janette and Erica were full of excitement, anticipating the fun they would have gliding down the hill on the plastic sleds we had purchased in Poland. Ed stood beside the car, waiting for Alicia to change into her warm outdoor clothing.

Within a couple of minutes, someone came running up the hill to tell Ed that Janette had been hurt. *No doubt a broken arm or leg,* he thought as he hurried toward her. When he arrived on the scene, however, he realized it was much more than a broken leg. Janette had flown down the hill, and her sled had failed to stop before the edge of the street. In what seemed to be a few split seconds of unfortunate timing, she slid under the wheels of a large truck. Ed found her crumpled body lying in the middle of the snowy street in a pool of blood. It is a scene Ed cannot erase from his mind, and it will haunt him for the rest of his life. In the days and years following the tragedy, I am thankful that, at least, I was spared that horror.

As Ed's confused mind tried to grasp the reality of the situation, several church friends and missionaries who were close by jumped into action. Someone had the presence of mind to stop Alicia from approaching the street. They led her and several other missionary children to a nearby apartment. A couple of college students gently carried Janette into the school to the nurse's station. Someone else called an ambulance. However, the emergency service was extremely unreliable, and even though the ambulance station was only a mile away, the ambulance never came. We couldn't imagine why this oversight happened and never received an explanation. Eventually, Valodia, Twila (a trauma nurse), Ed, and two of our college students, Sergei and Tolik, carried Janette to Valodia's car and drove her to the hospital.

Ed remembers glancing into the back seat of the car where Janette was laying across the laps of Sergei and Tolik. He caught a glimpse as one of them gently closed Janette's eyes. Those beautiful eyes! Pain stabbed at his heart.

From the moment Janette was born, her eyes captivated everyone. I will forever remember the nurse placing her gently in my arms as the beautiful sunset streamed rays of orange and red through the hospital window. Her irises were a stunning sapphire encircled with a wide, darker ring that accentuated the beautiful blue. When Ed or I took her shopping, people would coo over our sweet baby and exclaim, "She has such big, beautiful eyes!" As she grew older, her insatiable zest for life bubbled up and sparkled in her eyes, making them even more attractive. We became accustomed to the comments from friends and strangers, but once she could understand, I silently hoped people wouldn't say anything. I wanted her to be known for her inner grace not her physical beauty. Now, the life had gone out of those beautiful eyes. They were closing for the last time. In that moment, Ed grasped the finality of the situation.

When they arrived at the hospital, the staff immediately whisked Janette off to another room. Our Ukrainian friends took charge of filling out the necessary reports. Ed sat on a simple wooden chair along the wall in the hallway. He was exhausted in body and spirit. After a while, Twila came out into the hallway. She immediately grew alarmed. Ed was extremely pale. His hands were beginning to curl involuntarily. These symptoms were a clear indication that Ed's body was going into shock. Twila flew into action. She instructed the nursing staff to hydrate him as quickly as possible. They brought him water and moved him to a hospital room where he could be monitored.

They feared that Ed might die, too.

Looking back, everyone had good reason to be fearful of Ed's well-being. He was saying things people say when they are near death. Ed told Sergei that Jesus was in the room and that he saw angels. He apparently said other things, too, but Sergei chose to keep those revelations to himself. Finally, the nurses gave Ed some bitter-tasting medicine to sedate him.

By the time I arrived, Ed was stabilized and appeared to be out of danger. The medicine had done its work, and he was resting. I spoke with Sergei who had stayed by his side the entire time. He told me that Ed had given him a real scare with his visions. He was relieved and grateful when his condition improved. Ed has always been so grateful for Sergei's gentle and comforting spirit. Sergei's care for Ed sustained him and kept him connected to earth during that time of acute shock and emotional pain.

Soon, our good friends and colleagues Melvin and Sandy Adams arrived. Melvin was the director of our organization's ministry in Ukraine. I will never be able to express how much their friendship and leadership has meant to us, especially during this critical time in our lives. Even though I know our tragedy also touched their family deeply, they often carried us when we were incapable of moving forward. Their strength upheld us.

After a few words of condolence, Melvin carefully broached

the subject of what our plans would be. Would we have a funeral in Ukraine? Would we go back to the United States or Canada? Even though we were reeling from the events of the day, I believe God gave Ed and I both clarity on what would be our best move. We agreed that we would take Janette's body back to Canada and have a funeral surrounded by our family.

Not only did we need our family, but they also needed us. We knew it was important for them to have the opportunity to comfort us and experience closure. No doubt our decision increased the legal work for Melvin and Valodia. But they both graciously accepted our decision and began the process of arranging travel for our family and procuring the necessary paperwork for the international transport of Janette's body.

Melvin and Sandy insisted we stay with them in their home that night. Even though we had not considered it, this proved to be a wise decision. Alicia was already there when we arrived at the apartment, and several friends had gathered to be with us in our grief. But our first thought was to comfort Alicia and to confirm that Janette had died and was now with Jesus. We held each other and cried together. Melvin called our parents. We had no strength left to make those difficult calls.

After a short visit with our concerned friends, we went to bed. Ed's sedative took effect, and he was soon asleep. Alicia's bed was on the floor beside me. Neither of us fell off to sleep quickly. We cried and held hands in the darkness.

I believe it is in God's wise providence that He does not reveal our future ahead of time. If I had realized the extent of the arduous journey of grief that was beginning for me that night, it may have discouraged me from getting up in the morning and taking the next feeble step forward. Instead, God, in loving mercy and grace, only asks that we take one day at a time, and He promised that "as thy days so shall thy strength be" (Deut. 33:25). Somehow, I knew I was going to lean hard on Him for strength in the coming days.

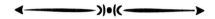

Reflecting on Your Journey

Who supported you in your darkest hour?

Where did you find the strength to keep going when it seemed impossible?

3

DOES GOD'S CALL INCLUDE THIS?

When you do good and suffer, if you take it patiently, this is commendable before God.
—I Peter 2:20

Within days of Janette's death, we heard comments and questions from our Ukrainian friends that went something like this: "I don't understand how God could allow this to happen to you. You gave up so much to come as missionaries. Why has He allowed this tragedy?"

We heard the same questions from our American and Canadian friends. We didn't have an answer. But in our hearts, we knew we didn't go to Ukraine to escape hardship and suffering. We went expecting hard times. By the time of Janette's death, we had already endured hardship and loss. But did we expect to sacrifice our daughter? *No. Obviously not.*

We had no idea what we would face, but we went with the knowledge that God was with us. Accepting the fact that there would be hardships when following God's call made us strong enough to endure those situations when we would inevitably experience them.

In the fall of 1993, Ed and I were certain God was calling us as missionaries to Ukraine. It was a deep, strong call we each felt separately—before we had any knowledge God was speaking to the other. When we finally talked about it together, we marveled that we were both settled in our minds that this was the direction we should take. We never agonized over the decision. We just moved forward with confidence that God had laid this burden on our hearts.

By the summer of 1994, we were approved by the missions board, so we resigned our pastorate, sold our home, secured visas, and raised financial support. We sorted our belongings and packed eight large pieces of luggage for the trip to Ukraine.

We always knew this day would eventually come. Ed was finally realizing the fulfillment of God's call on his life, the clear missionary call he first heard as a single student in Bible college.

Ed never wavered from this unmistakable commission to God's service, and I have often referred to this as Ed's *general call*. But since I never experienced God speak to me in that way, I wondered, *Should I marry him when I don't have a similar call to be a missionary?* We discussed this before we were married and sought God's direction.

Admittedly, in those days, I had a rather narrow understanding of how God called people to commit themselves to Christian service. I thought every person who was called to missionary service would experience this type of grand awakening, which seemed to me rather mysterious. As I wrestled through this in my mind, I heard a veteran missionary speak about his life. He shocked everyone by saying he never had a call. Instead, he simply surrendered his entire life to Christ and was willing to go wherever God led him.

That moment changed my perspective. It seemed God said to me, "Are you willing to go anywhere I ask?" I answered with certainty, *Yes, Lord,* and from that moment, my heart was settled. I knew Ed and I would go wherever God led us. Anywhere. No reservations. I never imagined my decision could be that simple. So, when we felt

God directing us to Ukraine, we did not hesitate. We were sure it was the place God had chosen for us after years spent waiting for His direction.

We experienced many losses as we prepared to go to Ukraine. In fact, the entire process of preparing for the mission field was a continuous lesson in losing all those things that had, until then, been important in our lives.

Every missionary goes through this process.

We quit our jobs and say goodbye to our co-workers. Often, it is a job we love, so we find it difficult to leave. We grieve the loss of a familiar, rewarding, and predictable life. For many, this is a loss of identity. We are no longer a senior pastor or an account executive. Everything we have strived for is left behind as we find ourselves at square one again.

Not only do we experience a loss of identity, but we also experience a loss of security. Nothing gives us more security than having our own home, no matter how simple it may be. But to be ready for the mission field, we give up our home. We pack our belongings and place them in storage. We agonize over what to do with sentimental items. Then we load up a van to travel around the country to share our vision with interested church congregations. It may seem glamorous, but missionaries in this stage of preparation are basically homeless and stripped of security.

Don't misunderstand me. We did all this willingly and joyfully because we were confident in God's call and His promise of provision for us.

Probably the most difficult loss we experienced was the sudden absence of strong relationships that we had enjoyed over the years. We said goodbye to church friends and neighbors. Tears spilled out unbidden as we hugged our parents, siblings, and other family members before crossing the barrier and stepping into the security area at the airport. Our hearts were heavy. *Would we ever see them again?* Everything familiar was being stripped away.

Then we turned our faces with inward resolve toward the country of our calling. We embraced the challenges of the unknown: a new land with strange customs and the challenge of ministering to people of a different culture.

It was no surprise to us that missionary life was hard. We expected to face hardships. Isn't that what everyone worries about? We sing, "Please Don't Send Me to Africa," and even though it is a light-hearted song, we do secretly hope we won't be asked to give up our comfortable life for the challenges of living in a different culture with "lions, gorillas, or snakes."

We felt a generous amount of apprehension mixed with our commitment to missionary service. We knew about the food shortages and even physical attacks on missionaries in Ukraine. Three months before our scheduled departure, Melvin Adams was robbed and beaten within an inch of his life. We knew of the dangers, but it did not change our commitment to follow God's leading.

Even though we expected life to be difficult, we had no way of knowing the specific hardships we would face. We had heard about culture shock, which is the experience of losing everything familiar and having it replaced by everything unfamiliar. The minute we stepped onto foreign soil we found ourselves groping in the darkness of the unknown. We could not communicate with people and became like kindergarten children again, learning to read strange-looking letters and phrases. It was difficult to put our thoughts into words, and we stammered and stumbled over the nuances and sounds of the language.

We also had to learn a whole new way of shopping. Gone were the beautiful, clean, well-stocked supermarkets; instead, we had outdoor markets where people brought their home-grown produce, meat, sour cream, and cottage cheese. Items were placed on a small table or on a blanket on the ground. Some vendors made trips to Poland to bring back a variety of miscellaneous household and clothing items. I found shopping extremely disorganized and confusing.

Ed had an easier time. His adventurous spirit made him more suited to that type of shopping, so he helped me out until I adapted to the market.

I remember other losses, too. Methods of communication with our family and friends in Canada and the United States were poor, and the distance seemed greater than ever. My mother wrote to us every week, but it took six weeks for us to receive her letters. Even though they took so long to arrive, they were a lifeline for us, and we looked forward to receiving those handwritten pages filled with news from home.

We adjusted to curfews, a holdover from the Soviet regime, that restricted our freedom. No one was allowed to leave or enter the city limits after ten at night. Every road in and out of the city was monitored by police checkpoints, and the police officers detained anyone according to their wishes. They were not known for their understanding or for giving travelers the benefit of the doubt. This required us to plan our trips carefully, especially when visiting missionary colleagues who lived in another part of the city. The route to their house took us briefly outside the city limits. If we failed to leave their place early enough in the evening, we risked the chance of being stopped on our return to the city limits after curfew.

Yes, we suffered losses, but I must also mention the incredible gains. When we arrived in the country of our calling, we recognized definite gains, which helped to ease the void that the losses left in our hearts. We developed new, strong relationships with both missionaries and national people. Some of these relationship bonds have endured the test of time. Gradually, appreciation for some of the ways of life in our new country grew, and we enjoyed a broader outlook on life. We also realized the satisfaction of fulfilling God's call on our lives and accomplishing things of eternal value.

Our tragedy happened while we were obeying God's call to a foreign field. When we answered God's call, we didn't bargain with Him that we would only go if He promised everything would be rosy. That deal would've been presumptuous and silly. When we accepted God's call, we knew we would be stretched to the limit, to the point it might seem like all our dreams were being destroyed.

Though some felt it was unfair we had to face such a deep, painful trial, we already knew following God's call would include loss and suffering. That awareness prepared us to weather the immediate shock and strengthened us to face the months and years to come.

All of us, at some time in our lives, will experience the give and take of losses and gains. However, some losses make it difficult to see any redemptive reason for the pain. Terminal illness, disability, divorce, abuse, business failure, and untimely deaths are all losses that fit this category. When we experience these types of losses, we find ourselves on a journey of grief that takes emotional strength and stamina to survive.

The scripture says it is commendable to endure our suffering patiently. That isn't always easy, but we need to cling to God's faithfulness and trust He is doing something special in our lives—even in difficult seasons that require exceptional perseverance.

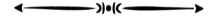

Reflecting on Your Journey

Have you been tempted to think it is unfair to suffer when trying to serve God faithfully?

Did you expect to avoid all hardship because of your commitment to God?

4

AN UNEXPECTED HARVEST

You do not know what will happen tomorrow.
—James 4:14

A split-second tragedy that takes a child's life has a way of vividly reminding us of the frailty and brevity of life.

We all know life is fragile and brief, but we live with that knowledge somehow pushed to the back of our minds. We live as if we will never die. In some ways, this is good. We need to make long-term plans and have dreams and aspirations. We cannot live our lives in fear of dying tomorrow, but we do need to be reminded that we are not promised a long life or even another day.

When I was seven years old, my world was rocked when a teenage neighbor had a fatal motorcycle accident on the corner in our subdivision. We could look out our dining room window and practically see the corner. It was that close to our home.

Randy's family lived two houses down from our family, and all the kids on the block played together and attended the same school. His sister was one of my close friends. When Randy got his driver's license, he bought a motorcycle. He hadn't had it long when he came to the corner in our subdivision and pulled out in front of an oncoming truck. Either he didn't see the truck, or he misjudged how much time he had to pull out and get in front of it. We will never know.

This event left me with a strong aversion to motorcycles, which I have to this day. A few times during our marriage, Ed has tossed around the idea of buying a motorcycle as a cheap form of transportation. Even though I know he would be careful, I cannot overcome my fear that he would come to an early death. While he does not fully understand my fear, he has honored my wishes and has never bought one.

I remember going to Randy's funeral and the strange heaviness I felt. It was the first funeral I ever attended. Even at that young age, I realized how quickly someone could be snatched from their family and friends. I saw the pain on his parents' faces and the sorrow in the eyes of his siblings. His family never seemed the same again. I felt a certain heaviness when I was around them, and since experiencing my own loss, I better understand their emotions.

Another tragedy struck our community about five years later. A couple of my school friends were walking along the edge of our country road at night. With no streetlights and no moonlight, it was pitch black. A light rain was falling. A car came from behind them, and the driver didn't see the young girls walking on the edge of the pavement until it was too late. The car hit one of the girls, and she was killed. The girl walking beside her, but closer to the shoulder of the road, was uninjured, though she struggled emotionally for a long time. Grief hung like a dark cloud over our school and community for weeks. The parents of the deceased girl withdrew from life, and I don't remember ever seeing them smile again.

For me, this seemed like tragedy upon tragedy. Even though I believe it is human to struggle with loss, I do not believe it should define our life. There is a healthy response to grief and an unhealthy response. Even today, I strive to find the delicate balance of grieving fully but not allowing myself to be defined by grief. It doesn't help anyone to let a loss, however great, rob us of our joy. Our family deserves better. We deserve better.

Within a day of Janette's accident, we began making plans to return to Canada for her funeral. With so many details to be worked out, we had a hard time making rational decisions. One of the symptoms of shock is brain fog; it's hard to think straight. This was true for us. Thankfully, Melvin and Valodia took care of many details for us, like arranging transportation of Janette's body to Canada and purchasing our plane tickets. Sandy fed and nurtured us while my parents in Canada took care of the funeral arrangements for us.

We were due for a home assignment in four months, so our initial plan was to go to Canada for the funeral and then return directly to Ukraine. But Melvin wisely advised us to take those extra months to adjust and plan our deputation, rather than return to Ukraine. Though we were not fully aware ourselves, he knew we would need the time for healing. Recovering from the tragedy would have been even more difficult, no doubt, if it was coupled with living under the stress of cultural hardships.

A memorial service was planned for Sunday evening in Kiev so the missionaries and our Ukrainian friends could pay tribute to Janette's life, express their condolences, and experience closure. I guess everyone pulled together on very short notice because within two days of the accident, we were attending a memorial service.

That evening, we entered the dingy school auditorium our mission rented for church services, a place we had entered many times before. But this time, it seemed so dreary. The dim lights failed to illuminate the dark corners of the room. Large, leaky windows lined two sides of the auditorium, and in a few places, the broken windows were patched with cardboard. The radiators along the walls fought unsuccessfully to pierce the cold with a bit of warmth. And as usual, we kept our winter coats, boots, gloves, and scarves on during the entire service in a feeble attempt to stay warm.

Janette's picture was displayed on a table at the front of the auditorium, along with a nice bouquet of artificial white flowers that I have kept to this day. I remember my first glimpse of her picture and the stab of pain that ripped at my heart. I diverted my eyes to help maintain my composure, and throughout the service, I avoided looking at the picture again.

The service consisted of various presentations and tributes. In addition, Ed said a few words during the service. He expressed how confident he was that God was good and still in control and that His plan was perfect. I confess, his glowing words landed like a thud on my heart. How could this be God's perfect plan? I just didn't feel it. In my *mind*, I knew God was always good. I had been taught this principle since I was a child and had memorized the scriptures that reinforced this truth. But, at that moment, my *heart* didn't feel it. The grief and pain were too acute. In the coming days and weeks, I would gradually get my heart to accept what I knew in my mind, but it did not happen immediately.

One thing I learned is that grief challenges our beliefs. Do we really believe Romans 8:28, that *all things work together for good for those who love God and are called according to His purpose? Do we really believe that God is all powerful and won't allow us to be given a heavier burden than we can carry? Do we really believe God will give us strength enough for every trial?*

When we face tragedy and grief, we must be firmly planted in God's Word and confident in our beliefs. Otherwise, the ground under us will be shaken and fall away.

Though so young, Janette had a huge impact on the people of Ukraine. She was a sincere, dedicated Christian—spiritual beyond her years. She did everything wholeheartedly, and her spiritual life was no different. She was serious about her devotion to God, and sometimes she put me to shame with her commitment to daily scripture reading, prayer journaling, and reaching out with compassion to others. Janette wasn't just a missionary *kid;* she was serious about being a missionary.

During the memorial service in Ukraine, many people came face to face with this reality: life is short, and it pays to be ready. At the close of the service, the altar was lined with seekers, and several made lifelong commitments to follow Christ. This harvest for God's kingdom helped us realize that her death was not in vain. It had eternal, lasting value. We had come to Ukraine to see a harvest of souls. We did not think it would take our daughter's death to see this happen, however, God used our tragedy to speak to the hearts of those who attended the service that evening. It provided some consolation to us that her life had produced fruit for the Kingdom, which is exactly what she lived for and the ultimate purpose of our missionary commitment. This experience gave us the courage to lift our eyes above the earthly pain and catch a glimpse of heavenly glory.

Reflecting on Your Journey

What have you done to keep your grief from defining you?

Have you seen any redemptive purpose in your tragedy?

5

SEARCHING FOR ANSWERS

I have learned that faith means trusting in advance what will only make sense in reverse.
—Philip Yancey

The world is full of people who have experienced pain, loss, sadness and trauma. Every day the news is filled with tragic events that we cannot comprehend. We see pictures of starving children with spindly arms and legs and protruding bellies living in countries racked by famine and drought. We read the story of a young girl who has been kidnapped, hidden in a cellar, and continuously abused for years. Our hearts grow heavy with knowing these traumas happen, but we are powerless to change the outcome.

Terrorist attacks on innocent people are particularly difficult to understand. I remember visiting the memorial of the Oklahoma City bombing, a senseless attack in 1995 on a federal building in Oklahoma. The memorial consists of rows of chairs, each one representing a life that was lost; the smaller chairs are a painful reminder of the children who lost their lives in the explosion. Viewing the memorial was an intensely sobering experience. I wondered, *What possesses people to commit such horrendous acts, and how do we, who are left behind, recover from tragedy, sorrow and loss?*

Ed and I experienced our own times of questioning as we walked through the deep valley of sorrow in the days following Janette's accident. *Why her? Why us?* Surely God could have made her hesitate or be distracted for a moment at the top of the hill. One brief minute of delay would have given space for the truck to avoid her sled. How could all the variables align so precisely as to put her in the street directly under the truck at that split second, thus creating this tragedy? It all seemed like a dreadful twist of fate. Why didn't a moment's pause or a slowing of the truck spare us such a devastating outcome? Many times, we have faced an unexpected delay and later realized it probably saved us from possible calamity. *Why didn't God do it for Janette that day?*

This brings us back to the age-old question: why does God allow bad things to happen to good people? Countless theologians have tried to provide rational answers to satisfy this question. I have read what many of them have had to say.

But to be transparent, I still do not know why God allows bad things to happen to good people. I don't know why cancer strikes innocent children or why a husband cheats on his wife and then leaves her broken emotionally and financially. I don't know why some women miscarry their babies, smashing their hopes and dreams for the future. The truth is that no one knows. We are not God. Only He knows.

Some would argue that we shouldn't ask why when we are faced with situations we don't understand. Somehow, they believe it is an affront to God and shows a lack of trust on our part. But, during our grief journey, I came to terms with the question and realized wondering why is okay. However, I also realized I had to be content with the fact that I would never get a satisfactory answer. I'm human, and it is human for us to wonder about things we do not understand. But I cannot expect or demand that God reveal His divine plan to me. God is not required to speak to me and give His reasons for allowing our daughter to be snatched from us at the young age of eleven. He is not required to tell me why Alicia should have to go through life without the friendship and companionship of a sister. He is not required to tell me why He has allowed us to go through this deep valley of grief and pain. I cannot demand that He answer my questions.

When I came to terms with this truth, it helped me find peace. I realized that it is normal for me to have questions. In our humanity, we're curious and wonder about things that are beyond our comprehension. Thankfully, God understands I cannot simply put questions out of my mind by the sheer force of my will and pretend I have no questions. He knows there are times in my life when I wonder about issues and events that have taken place. But I also know that, in the end, God asks me to be content with the mystery of not knowing. I need to rest in the assurance that, although we see through a glass darkly in this life, the answer will someday be revealed to us (1 Cor. 13:12).

Some well-intentioned people tried to offer us answers—no doubt because they were also wrestling with the question. But none provided me with much satisfaction because I knew God's plan was deeper and broader than our imaginations.

One answer offered was that God knew He could trust us with such a deep trial, as if somehow it was a badge of honor—a sign of our spiritual strength—to experience such a tragedy. This explanation only increased my pain. *Was I being punished because I trusted God fully? If I was weaker spiritually or had lived a less committed life, would I have avoided this?*

I don't believe God only gives us what we can handle. I believe he helps us handle what we are given. Perhaps, like Job, we were being tested to see if we would be faithful even through great loss, but I found it easier to live with no answer than to grapple with this possible answer. If our tragedy was a test from God, then so be it, and I was willing to pass the test. However, I preferred not to view it as such.

Another possible answer was spiritual warfare, that Satan was trying to thwart our ministry. Even if this wasn't the reason for our tragedy, I'm sure it was true. In the months leading up to the accident, we faced several incidents we recognized as oppression and opposition from Satan. In fact, we wrote a newsletter to our family and friends outlining some of our negative experiences and asked them to pray for us. It seemed that every way we turned; something was going wrong. Looking back, of course, we realize that those experiences were not all that distressing compared to the loss of Janette's life. But at the time, we knew we were shining the light of the Gospel in an area of the world where Satan had held a tight grip for many years, and he was fighting our efforts. Even so, this explanation did not answer the question of why God allowed her death. Other missionaries were also serving in Ukraine, and not all of them experienced what we experienced. We do not know why we were chosen for this crisis.

Another possible explanation was that "God was working all things together for our good" (Rom. 8:28) and that somehow this tragedy was necessary for us to experience the "goodness" God envisioned for us. Even though I believe God wants what is best for his children, I had a difficult time seeing the *good* in our tragedy. A deeper look at Romans 8:28 brought me to the conclusion that a better understanding of this verse is, "God works in all things."

If we believe this, we can accept that God has chosen to work in a context where He does not exclude the possibility of events that are hurtful to believers. However, we can be assured He will work on our behalf to help us through any difficulties we may face, and if we cooperate with Him, we can turn our painful experiences into opportunities for growth. After all, the ultimate goal is that we "be conformed to the image of Christ" (Rom. 8:29).

If we are going to have victory in the midst of circumstances we cannot explain, we must avoid seeing ourselves as victims. It is easy to get so caught up in the misery of our situation that we fail to realize that we should expect to have difficulty and trials. Scripture reminds us that in this world we will have tribulation (John 16:33), so we should not be surprised by it.

The day after the accident, we had a visit from the police to get our report, and they urged us to press murder charges. We were adamant: it was an accident. No amount of punishment for the truck driver would bring her back. It was true the driver was going the wrong way on a narrow one-way street, so he was breaking the law. Our position was that the police could charge him for a traffic violation, but we did not see that charging him for murder would help anyone. Yes, he made a serious mistake, but he did not deliberately kill our daughter. She slid under his truck without him even knowing it happened. No doubt his mental torment would be punishment enough. Besides, we were guests in a foreign country, and we did not want to become embroiled in a legal battle.

Within a few hours after the police left, the driver also came to visit us. Ed and Melvin talked with him. I lacked the energy to even come out of my room. Ed told him he forgave him, and we wouldn't be pressing charges. He told him God was a forgiving God and we hoped he would seek forgiveness from God and find peace. Melvin followed up with him over the course of several months and reported to us that he led him to Christ. Unfortunately, the Ukrainian people took matters into their own hands and continually shunned him. It was necessary for him to move several times because when people discovered he had killed a child, they were hostile to him. We lost track of him but continued to pray he would follow God completely.

If we are going to survive the journey of grief, we will have to defeat the "Why me?" syndrome. We will also have to surrender our desire to seek revenge, to hurt the other person so they will also feel pain. In fact, obsession with punishing the other person can consume us. Unless we relinquish our desire to ease our pain by demanding punishment, we will only drag ourselves down.

I once read the story of a man who lost several family members in a car accident. A drunk driver swerved into oncoming traffic and hit his family head-on. When the driver went to trial, his lawyer was shrewd and convinced the jury it was possible his client was not the one driving the vehicle. In the end, the driver got off the hook with no charges. The man who lost his family recounted how the verdict consumed him night and day for many months. He eventually realized how important it was for him to have someone pay for the crime. It was only when he released the outcome to God that he finally found peace.

I am forever grateful we chose that path of acceptance from the beginning. It saved us additional torment and heartache in trying to control what we could not control.

Do not misunderstand what I am saying. I am not implying there should be no justice for crimes. I am only pointing out that we need to avoid becoming invested in legal battles that do not bring healing and rest to our souls. This is not easy, and sometimes it calls for conscious choices that go against our natural human impulses. Having the courage to make those choices can bring private victories, making the journey grief more bearable.

Reflecting on Your Journey

Have you ever felt guilty questioning God about your hardship or tragedy?

Have you learned to be okay without knowing the answers to your questions?

Have you relinquished your desire to seek revenge on the one who hurt you?

6

IN THE NICK OF TIME

*My grace is sufficient for you, for my strength is made
perfect in weakness.*
—2 Corinthians 12:9

The day after the memorial service, we awoke to the monumental task of securing our home in Ukraine for the months we would be away. Under normal circumstances, we would spend several weeks in preparation, arranging for a trustworthy person to watch our home and making sure other responsibilities were covered.

Who would be responsible to submit payments for our ongoing expenses in our absence? Where would we park our car so someone could watch to make sure it was safe? Who would be responsible for our teaching and ministerial duties? Who would check the pipes in our home? What if they froze in the cold weather? Who would pick up our mail at the post office? All these duties flooded our minds.

Besides these details, we needed to sort our clothes and pack necessities for an extended absence. But my mind was numb. It was hard to think or make decisions. Thankfully, several missionary women came to help us pack and make sense of the many details that crowded our thoughts. They shared our grief as we organized our lives for the days ahead. We so deeply appreciated their care for us in that chaotic time.

While we were packing, Twila said to me, "Heather, I want you to know that Janette died instantly." I stared at her blankly as I tried to comprehend her words and process this information. But I could only manage to nod my head and continue to pack. My thoughts were so scattered that, only later, when I started to sift through the events of those tragic days, was I able to fully understand her comment's meaning and significance. When my mind cleared, I found consolation in knowing Janette did not suffer. She was instantly gathered into the arms of Jesus. She was safe. She was at peace.

The realization Janette died instantly not only helped me find healing for my grief, but it also better prepared me for mission work in the less fortunate countries of our world.

Let me explain. As I mulled over the facts and details of that sad afternoon, I could not comprehend why the ambulance never came to the scene of the accident. *How could the medical personnel be so callous as not to respond to our call for help?*

Our Ukrainian friends were not surprised by this neglect. Ambulance drivers in Ukraine often did not respond to calls of distress. Our friends told us that perhaps the ambulance wouldn't start or was out of gas. Or maybe the paramedics had grown tired of, once again, searching their bare cupboards for food and looking at the hungry faces of their wives and children. Their families often went hungry because the communist government had not paid them for weeks. So, perhaps they had siphoned gas out of the ambulance and sold it to feed their families.

Somewhat comforted in knowing that Janette had died instantly, I gradually came to have deeper compassion for the people of Ukraine. Instead of being bitter toward the ambulance drivers, I could more fully understand how the communist way of life had robbed the people of their basic human dignity. The Ukrainian culture was being bankrupted by ruthless leaders who put no value on human life.

My own experiences were starting to break down the barriers between myself and the Ukrainian people. If I were to be victorious over my own biases, and more fully enter into a life of service to others, I needed to accept the full reality of life in Ukraine and not place blame, especially when I didn't know the reasons—whether those reasons were right or wrong, good or bad. This was a critical step in my development as a missionary.

To be able to overcome the obstacles I would face in the future, I needed to unreservedly love, at the deepest level of my being, the Ukrainian people and all other humans we would meet in our ministry, wherever God would send us. Otherwise, I would fail in my attempts to let God use me on the mission field. This wholehearted commitment to love all God's children had to come from the deepest part of my being. This was something I had to simply accept as part of the sacrifice I made in order to follow God without reservation.

Where do we get the grace to handle these seemingly impossible circumstances? Our own experience helps me answer this question. Immediately following the accident, Ed and I were amazed at the grace and strength God gave us to remain strong despite the circumstances. As events unfolded day by day, we were given the supernatural power we needed to survive our tragedy.

I believe we receive this grace by unreservedly relying on God and allowing Him to give us this grace. If you had told me before the accident that I was going to face the death of my young daughter, I would have said I did not have enough grace for that. Surely, I would fall apart! I would be crushed under such a burden. But in the moment of our greatest need, God's grace kept pace with what we were asked to bear. We get grace when we need it—not before we need it. I like to say, *God's grace is always there in the nick of time. Never early. Never late. Always on time. And always enough.*

Recently, I understood this truth even more clearly while reading Mark 6. The sky grew dark, and the disciples frantically struggled with the unruly oars and sails as the wind whipped around them.

They feared the little fishing boat would capsize in the sea's angry waves, and that is when Jesus came walking to them on the water: *during* the storm. He did not come to them when the sea was calm and the skies were blue. He came when they were at the end of their human capabilities and fearful for their lives. Because they had spent time with Him, they knew everything would be all right once Jesus arrived on the scene. It is the same way in our lives when we are thrust into a deep trial. God will show up with the grace and help we need. He won't give it before we need it, but it will be on time.

What will grace do for us? Grace gives us the power to choose a positive response to our situation. It provides the ability to yield to God's perfect plan and submit to His direction. Grace gives us the courage to resist the temptation to become self-centered and think our pain is worse than others. Through grace, we find strength to discover God's redemptive purposes in our suffering.

For me to remain centered in God's care and maintain a positive spirit during my heartache, it was necessary to look at some things objectively. One way that helped put my situation into perspective and kept me from sinking into the depths of despair was to ask myself, *How could our situation be worse?*

At first, I could not think of anything worse than Janette's tragic death. But gradually, I began to see her death through clearer eyes. If we had been asked to watch our child die of cancer, that would be worse. The slow, agonizing process of watching a child die must be worse than having her die without suffering. The only blessing of a slower death is less shock and a little more time to prepare emotionally for inevitable grief. However, the loss is the same. As I weighed this possibility, I realized it was probably better in our situation to avoid a lengthy sickness, especially in a country with low medical standards.

Another situation I thought about was kidnapping. It must be incredibly painful for parents to wonder where their child is and how she is being treated. *Is she suffering? Is she being beaten or sexually abused? Is she alive or dead?* The pain of not knowing must be torture to the heart of a parent. The constant wondering during every waking moment and endless sleepless nights would be painful beyond imagination. I decided that knowing my child's fate and knowing she had not suffered was better than the uncertainty of such a scenario. At least we had a semblance of closure.

By asking, *What could be worse?* I discovered I was less likely to feel self-pity. Instead, I was thankful for some of the things I did not have to endure, things like uncertainty and extended suffering. Are these situations worse than what I experienced? I don't know because that wasn't my journey. I only know that thinking about those possibilities helped me to have a less painful response to my situation.

My specific trial had come without warning, and I was crushed under the pressure. I found myself on a dark and lonely path. But God's grace gave me the strength to submit to the stretching of my ability to trust God, and to discover His redemptive purposes for my pain.

Like the disciples, I had to lift my eyes from my storm-filled situation and look to Jesus to immerse myself in the deep waters of God's grace. This was the only way I could live through the pain of Janette's death. I had to respond with complete trust in God and allow Him to give me the confidence and hope to persevere.

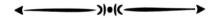

Reflecting on Your Journey

What special grace have you needed along your journey of grief?

What did you do to keep yourself from self-pity?

Was God's grace stronger than you could have anticipated?

7

FINDING MY WAY IN THE DARK

The darkest moments of our lives are not to be buried and forgotten, rather they are a memory to be called upon for inspiration to remind us of the unrelenting human spirit and our capacity to overcome the intolerable.
—Vince Lombardi

It's typical for missionaries to look forward to their time away from the mission field with great anticipation. They dream about reuniting with family and friends and enjoying the warmth of those familiar relationships. They anticipate backyard barbeques and comfortable conversations free from the stress of worrying about personal safety. They look forward to visiting their favorite restaurants and enjoying the luxury of being served. Women often look forward to the ease of shopping in a well-stocked grocery store or spending an afternoon leisurely walking through a mall.

None of these thoughts entered our minds as we traveled to the airport to leave Ukraine and fly to New York. Instead of having something to look forward to, we were facing the trip with dread.

Several of our Ukrainian and missionary friends gathered at the Kiev airport to say good-bye and show their love and support. Their care and concern touched us deeply. After hugs and tearful good-byes, we once again turned our faces with all the courage we could muster toward the long terminal corridor that would lead to our gate.

During this time, I experienced memory loss that was very uncommon for me: *Where are our passports? Where did I put that credit card?* I had been the person who knew exactly where everything was all the time. I could pack eight seventy-pound suitcases, and if Ed wanted something, I knew which suitcase and where inside it the item could be found. Now, I could not even remember what I had done with our passports an hour ago. Everything was happening so fast that I felt like I was losing touch with my life. It seemed like I had stepped onto a roller coaster that was propelling me—against my will—to go faster than I wanted to go. Everything was a blur. There was an uncomfortable feeling in the pit of my stomach that wouldn't go away.

We boarded the plane and settled into our seats. There were announcements and cross-checks. Soon, we were taxiing and preparing for take-off. A strange mixture of emotions flooded over us, but during the next several hours, we had plenty of time for processing our thoughts. We were headed to our birth countries and to the arms of our families. We knew we needed their love and support more than ever. As reassuring as all that was, the reason for this unexpected trip hung like a shadow of pain as we made our journey home. We found short periods of sleep from sheer exhaustion, but at other times, tears spilled from our eyes and poured down our faces in the shadowy darkness of the plane's cabin. The reality of taking Janette home for her burial seemed too much to absorb. We kept realizing this difficult truth anew as it sank into our thoughts and our consciousness.

Finally, we landed in New York City, and our brother-in-law, Robert, was there to accompany us on our final flight to Syracuse, New York. Although it was technically not necessary for him to meet us in New York City, it was such a comfort to have him with us, to assist us as we navigated the massive JFK airport and waited for our flight. We were exhausted physically and emotionally. Robert's kind, thoughtful gesture lightened our load.

As I think back to that difficult time, Robert's kindness challenges me to be more aware of creative ways I can help others who are facing times of grief and sadness. It reminds me of the old saying, "Everyone wants to be the sunshine to brighten up someone's life; why not be the moon to shine on someone's darkest hour?"

We landed in Syracuse, and our small plane parked a short distance from the terminal. It was night-time. We were on the last flight of the day, and the starless sky hung deep and cold over the winter night. Steps led across the tarmac to the airport entrance. Our parents and a few family members stood by the terminal windows. As we walked to meet them, a new and painful reality struck us. We were arriving home as a family of three, not four. Janette's grandparents were seeing our family for the first time without her.

Ed felt a keen responsibility for not bringing Janette back with us alive. In his mind, he had failed them. He was the one who felt responsible for their grief. These ideas and similar thoughts tormented him over the coming months and years.

During the grieving process, we all have irrational thoughts and beliefs. For many people, grief takes the form of self-blame. But Janette's death was not Ed's fault. Nothing he could have done would have protected her from this accident, yet he blamed himself. This is a common, yet anguished, response to loss.

Children sometimes blame themselves for their parents' divorce when everyone knows it is not their fault. Parents blame themselves for their children's wrong choices and wonder where they failed; they ask, *How could I have prevented them from choosing a life of crime or drugs?* Most of these thoughts are irrational, but the grieving mind plays games with us, and sometimes the pain obscures our ability to think rationally.

Of course, no one in our family blamed Ed for Janette's tragic accident. They welcomed us with open arms, warm hugs, tears, and comforting words. They made sure we had everything we needed and took care of most of the details for the funeral. Having a family with a strong faith in God carried us through the coming days.

Hundreds of friends and family came to the visitation to express their condolences. It was during this time I sensed another degree of memory loss that frightened me. I couldn't recognize people that, on one level, I had known so well, but as they approached me, my mind was blank. One couple who had visited Ukraine a few months earlier and spent time with us came to the visitation, and I had to search my brain to remember who they were. And although my memory has improved with the passing of the years, part of my memory bank has never recovered. It is one of the ways the trauma has changed me forever.

As Ed and I stood beside Janette's casket and said our last goodbyes at the funeral home just before going to the church, our missionary president, Gerald Bustin, slipped up beside us. Ed's simple words to him were, "No regrets." Having no regrets did not mean we were inoculated against the sharp pain and grief that gripped our hearts. Having no regrets did not mean we didn't wish somehow things were different, that we could awaken from this dreadful nightmare. Having no regrets simply meant we knew we had done our best.

We had poured our lives and our values into Janette from the time she was born. We had taught her to love and serve Jesus with her whole heart. We had been obedient to God's call and experienced the joy of serving Him wherever He chose to use us. Having no regrets meant the sacrifices were well worth the assurance we had, knowing she was at home, safe in heaven.

Janette was an avid reader. She liked reading biographies and true stories. About a year before her accident, she read Gerald Bustin's book *Teenage Missionary*. After reading the book, she announced that she planned to someday be a missionary to a primitive culture—preferably in a country where people had never heard the Gospel and lived in grass huts. But she wasn't waiting around for that elusive day to arrive. She was serious about being a missionary in Ukraine and always participated with enthusiasm in our various ministries.

She was captivated by the life and songs of Fanny Crosby, the blind girl who kept a beautiful spirit amid hardship and became a prolific hymn-writer. That is why we chose to have the congregation sing Fanny's well-known hymn "Blessed Assurance" at Janette's funeral.

Janette loved to sing. Every time her school had a talent night, she participated. The Christmas when she was seven, she charmed everyone with her strong performance of "All I Want for Christmas Is My Two Front Teeth." A few months later, she sang a captivating solo in an Easter production at her school, the second verse of "My Father's Angels." The picture of her singing this song, dressed as an angel, plays over in my mind every Easter as I think about the resurrection and I wonder, *What is Janette doing in heaven?*

A couple of weeks before her accident, we started making plans for our upcoming deputation. Janette had chosen a song she planned to sing with Alicia during the church services where we would represent our ministry. The song was "Live for Jesus" by Evie Tornquist-Karlsson. After her death, the words of this song took on new meaning.

> *Oh, I want to be remembered*
> *as the girl who sang her songs for Jesus Christ.*
> *Who was willing to lay down her life*
> *and do His will no matter what the price.*
> *Well, I am singing for the deaf man*
> *who can hear about salvation through my song,*
> *And I am singing for the blind man*
> *who can see the light in me and come along.*
>
> *Live for Jesus, that's what matters,*
> *And when other houses crumble mine is strong.*
> *Live for Jesus, that's what matters;*
> *That you see the light in me and come along.*
>
> *There are times when I am tempted to*
> *turn off this rugged road I've traveled on.*

> *There are times when I say,*
> *"Jesus can't you find another girl to sing your songs?"*
> *Well, I know it's not that I'm the only one*
> *who can sing this melody,*
> *But He's chosen me to bless me*
> *and to lead me into what is best for me.*
>
> *Live for Jesus, that's what matters,*
> *And when other houses crumble mine is strong.*
> *Live for Jesus, that's what matters;*
> *That you see the light in me and come along.**

Alicia sang this song as a solo in all the churches we visited that summer and fall. It was her testimony but also a tribute to Janette who had already surrendered everything to Jesus and was willing to lay down her life for the cause of Christ. It was how we raised our girls; with a high level of commitment to serving Jesus, regardless of the cost.

I am now on the other side of what has probably been my darkest hour, and I want to encourage those of you who are still facing days full of grief and despair. I understand it is terrifying to feel like your life is careening in a direction you don't want to go. It is difficult to keep hope alive and trust that the heaviness you feel will lighten. It is challenging to search for a ray of hope in the darkness of heartache and pain. Thankfully, God has promised that those who mourn will be comforted (Matt. 5:4). If we rest fully on His promises and patiently let Him fulfill His purpose in us, He will demonstrate His power through us to the world around us.

---

* "LIVE FOR JESUS" Words and Music by Nancy Henigbaum, Nancy © 1979 Curb Word Music (ASCAP) All rights administered by WC Music Corp.

Reflecting on Your Journey

What irrational thoughts crowded your mind in your time of grief?

Were you able to deal with those thoughts and get victory in those areas?

8

THIS DOESN'T CHANGE MY UNDERSTANDING OF GOD

Just because you can't see the air doesn't mean you stop breathing. And just because you can't see God doesn't mean you stop believing.
—Nicky Gumbel

The school in Windsor, Ontario, that Janette and Alicia attended before we began our missionary work in Ukraine planned a memorial service following the funeral. Normally, it was a six-hour drive from Kingston, Ontario, but in the snowy Canadian winter conditions, it stretched into eight hours of increased alertness. Even though I was accustomed to winter driving, I was a bundle of nerves as we traveled in blowing snow with poor visibility. Tragedy has a way of changing the way we react to otherwise normal situations, and I was experiencing the heightened sensitivities of grief. Thankfully, we made it safely, and I gathered my frazzled nerves to prepare for the service.

The students and teachers shared many memories and loving tributes about Janette. There were heartfelt prayers and encouraging scriptures, but what I remember most was that someone sang the song "Trust His Heart" by Babbie Mason. It was a relatively new song at the time, and this was the first time I heard it. The words spoke deeply to me and started me on a quest to reconcile my situation with the character of God.

> *All things work for our good,*
> *Though sometimes we don't see*
> *How they could.*
> *Struggles that break our hearts in two*
> *Sometimes blind us to the truth*
> *Our Father knows what's best for us*
> *His ways are not our own.*
> *So, when your pathway grows dim*
> *And you just don't see Him,*
> *Remember you're never alone.*
> *God is too wise to be mistaken,*
> *God is too good to be unkind,*
> *So, when you don't understand,*
> *When don't see His plan,*
> *When you can't trace His hand,*
> *Trust His Heart.*
> *Trust His Heart.*
> *He sees the master plan*
> *And he holds our future in His hand,*
> *So, don't live as those who have no hope,*
> *All our hope is found in Him.*
> *We see the present clearly,*
> *But He sees the first and the last.*
> *And like a tapestry He's weaving you and me,*
> *To someday be just like Him.*
> *God is too wise to be mistaken,*
> *God is too good to be unkind,*

> *So, when you don't understand,*
> *When don't see His plan,*
> *When you can't trace His hand,*
> *Trust His Heart.*†

As I heard this song, questions swirled in my head and settled in my heart: *Was God indeed too wise to be mistaken? How could this tragedy come from God's goodness?* It seemed to me that I had a huge knot in my tapestry rather than a beautiful, flowing design. *How could I reconcile my excruciating pain with my belief that God is all-powerful and could have prevented it?*

As humans, we do our best to avoid anything that will cause us pain or discomfort. Toddlers learn to keep their fingers away from the hot burner on the stove. Children try to please their parents to avoid the emotional pain that comes with disapproval. Teenagers try to fit in with their peers, so they won't feel the sting of rejection. As adults, we all tend to make decisions based on how comfortable the expected outcome will be for us. We are inclined to choose happiness, ease, and comfort rather than pain, hardship, and loss.

I admit our experience forced me to look at the character of God and not at the circumstances of life. When I looked at my situation from a human standpoint, it looked grim beyond comprehension. When I looked at my situation through the lens of God's character and eternal perspective, I knew I had to trust Him even when I did not understand His plan. What I had to accept was the fact that His wisdom and goodness make it impossible for Him to make a mistake that would cause me harm. Suffering is arduous, and our natural response is to seek relief as quickly as possible. However, if we ignore or numb the pain, we often miss out on healing and instead fall into hopelessness and bitterness. If we embrace our suffering and trust

---

† "TRUST HIS HEART" Words and Music by Eddie Carswell and Babbie Mason © 1989 Curb Word Music (ASCAP), May Sun Publishing (ASCAP) and Curb Dayspring Music (BMI) All rights on behalf of Curb Word Music and May Sun Publishing administered by WC Music Corp. All rights on behalf of Curb Dayspring Music administered by Warner-Tamerlane Publishing Corp.

that God is a loving Father who wants us to develop into a more tender child, our faith has a chance to grow.

> *Behold what manner of love the Father has bestowed on us,*
> *that we should be called children of God.*
> —1 John 3:1

Probably, like me, you've heard Bible teachers and preachers explain that our understanding of God is a mirror of how we relate to our earthly fathers. Thankfully, I had a wonderful dad who demonstrated loving authority, provision, and security to me from the time I was a little girl. He was kind, fun, generous, compassionate, and protective. He always had my best interest in mind and was a godly example in his faithful devotion to God. Oh, and he expected strict obedience. Consequently, it was easy for me to accept that God was a loving heavenly Father with whom I could share my joys and my sorrows. He would never do anything to hurt me—and He expects strict obedience.

At times while growing up, I could not understand why I was not allowed to do something fun or why my father required a specific action. If I asked, sometimes his answer was, "Because I said so." Maybe you heard this from your parents, too. I didn't like that response at the time, but looking back, I realize it taught me something very important. I learned to be obedient and accept my situation, even when I did not understand. Dad was the authority, and I needed to accept his wisdom and trust that he was looking out for my well-being. Not everything I wanted was good for me, even though I didn't understand why. I knew it was inconsistent with Dad's character to do something that would hurt me, so I needed to just *trust his heart*.

Even as wonderful as my earthly father was, he wasn't perfect. He made mistakes, like every human being does. In contrast, God is the *perfect* heavenly Father who does not make mistakes and whose love for us is not based on our performance or worthiness. His plans for us are always aimed at our ultimate benefit. He has the power and authority to accomplish what He knows is best for us. Learning to accept my earthly father's authority helped me accept God's sovereign authority amid what seemed to be twisted fate.

From the time I was a young girl in Sunday school, I studied the character of God: Infinite. All-Powerful. All-Knowing. Good. Kind. Unchanging. Omnipresent. Wise. Faithful. Just. Believing in a God with these wonderful character traits brought strength and stability to my faith.

So, what do we do when our circumstances collide with our understanding of the character of God? How can we reconcile that He is all powerful yet not demonstrating that power in the way we had hoped? Like most people who experience tragic loss, I wondered where God's power and goodness were when I needed them. Since the time of Janette's accident, I have heard many stories of how God miraculously spared other people's children from death. Of course, I rejoice with them, but I must be perfectly honest. I have sometimes wondered, *Where was our miracle? Why wasn't her life spared?*

Obviously, I do not expect to receive answers to these questions. Let's face it: God isn't required to let me know how His perfect plan all fits together. My frail mind could never hope to comprehend His sovereignty, anyway.

We see our lives from our human perspective, and our view is limited in its scope. We want to avoid hardship, pain, and loss. Like a child who wants to do something fun, we don't understand when God asks us to go through something difficult. But God has a much broader view, and He knows what is best for us in the long run. Usually, the reason for suffering is known only to God and remains a mystery to everyone else. Therefore, I think we should avoid trying to explain the reason for our suffering or the suffering of others. Instead, we must choose to trust His heart and believe that He knows best. Whether or not we understand His plan, we find immense peace in learning to trust when we don't understand. It is our way of cooperating with

Him as He conforms our will to His, and weaves our lives into His overall plan.

I draw a lot of strength from Mary, who watched her son die on a cross at the hands of the wicked mob. I cannot help but think she must have been questioning in her mind, *How can this be God's perfect plan? Isn't there another way? Why doesn't He call ten thousand angels and show His power?* Nevertheless, for some reason that we cannot comprehend, crucifixion was God's plan, and out of tragedy, God brought salvation to every man, woman, and child.

The choice seems clear to me: trust and have peace or question God's character and live in torment. If we cannot accept and reconcile our situation with the character of God, we will live our lives believing we are victims of bizarre circumstances. I prefer to accept that God is good and works everything together in our lives for His purpose—even when I can't trace His hand or see the beautiful tapestry He is weaving.

Reflecting on Your Journey

Have you struggled to reconcile your pain and the character of God?

Have you learned to trust His heart even when you don't understand?

9

SURROUNDED BY PRAYERS

Never underestimate the incredible power and tremendous blessing of prayer.
—Mark J. Musser

Whenever a tragic event occurs, the first thing people turn to is prayer. It is a natural human response. Even those who barely believe in God will cry out to Him when their life is in danger, or when someone close to them is facing a crisis. I've heard stories about people in the military who had no relationship with God, yet in the heat of battle, they instinctively prayed for safety.

Prayer is indeed powerful, and I am eternally grateful for those who prayed for us even when we could not pray for ourselves. As I look back on the immense emotional strength God gave me at the time of the accident, I realize that people were praying for me even before I heard the news—even people thousands of miles away!

As I shared earlier, because we did not have a phone, I was delayed in hearing about the accident. I learned later that Ed had also asked them to wait when asked if I should be contacted. In his mind, he wanted to protect me a little longer from the anguish he knew I would experience when I eventually heard the news.

At the time, his extending the delay caused me frustration. But I now see his choice gave time for the news to reach those who could immediately start praying for me. We know that over the next several weeks people who had never even met us prayed for us. We are so thankful for those prayers.

Our missionary colleagues and many of our Ukrainian friends had phones in their apartments. Several of them were at the scene when Janette was struck by the truck, and naturally, their first instinct was to spread the word and ask for prayer. When I finally pieced together the time frames, it occurred to me that my brother in Florida knew what had happened before I did!

While I was sitting at my kitchen table waiting and wondering, people around the world were already starting to pray *for me*. Could I have faced the immediate shock and been strong without those prayers? I don't know. I'm glad I did not have to find out.

Sometimes, when I relate this story to people, they are aghast that the proper chain of notification didn't take place that day. They imply that I should be upset by the lack of protocol in notifying the next of kin. Instead, I choose to see the silver lining in how the events unfolded and realize that I benefited by what I call "prayers in advance." Generally, there is more than enough blame to go around when tragedy strikes, and I prefer to avoid getting caught in that insidious trap.

I believe it was the prayers of our family and friends that carried us over the next several months. A few weeks after the funeral, we set out on a trip to Florida, where our mission organization was holding its annual camp meeting. We were emotionally drained, but we were pushing through and doing the next thing. Elizabeth Elliot says, "Sometimes life is so hard you can only do the next thing. Whatever it is, just do the next thing. God will meet you there."[1] We proved this to be true that weekend.

The long trip from Canada to Florida was one of the most difficult I remember us ever making. I wasn't sleeping well at night, so I was groggy during the day. Ed has always struggled to stay awake on long trips, so we played "driver tag" all the way. Toward the end of the trip, I remember switching drivers every fifteen minutes because neither of us could stay awake. It is frightening to find yourself waking up while driving!

Eventually, we found ourselves out in the middle of nowhere with no hotel to stop for the night. We had no cell phone, no data to search for hotels, and no GPS to encourage us that the minutes were ticking down. So, I used my flashlight to squint at the map, and we pushed on in the winter evening twilight by the sheer force of our wills to get to our destination.

Ed was looking forward to getting to the camp meeting because since the time of the funeral, he had been finding it increasingly difficult to pray. He says it wasn't that he blamed God. He just couldn't put thoughts together to form prayers. He would cry out to God, but he couldn't form a coherent prayer. This became a point of concern for him, and he longed to be able to communicate with God again. He felt confident he could get help at the camp meeting.

As soon as he found a good opportunity after our arrival, Ed asked some of the leaders to pray with him at the close of one of the services. Indeed, those spiritual giants stormed heaven on his behalf! From that time, he felt the brain fog lifting and his thoughts getting clearer. Once again, he was able to put his thoughts into prayers.

I want to underscore how important it is for us as the family of God to be serious about the privilege that is ours to pray for those who are facing a crisis. You never know. Maybe they are unable to pray for themselves. Your prayers can make a huge difference in their circumstances.

In this day of social media, the speed with which we can summon prayers amazes me. Hardly a day goes by that I don't see someone asking for prayer for a missing child, a tragic accident, a sick relative or a personal need. Truly, the internet is a great tool for communication, and it is wonderful that we can use it to bring prayers together quickly for various needs.

I think the danger, though, is that we tend to say a quick, superficial prayer when we see these posts, and we may even comment that we are praying. Then, we move on to the next post. We are bombarded by information overload in our online world, which means we can quickly forget the urgent needs.

Of course, I love pictures of grandchildren and posts about happy family times as much as anyone. They are always welcome in my newsfeed because these updates keep us connected and rejoicing with each other. But I have made it a point to remember throughout the day those who have asked for prayer because I know how important those prayers might be to them. Maybe they cannot pray for themselves. Maybe they find themselves staring at the impossible. Where will they get the strength to do the next thing? I believe they often find that strength from the prayers of others. I know we did.

Sometimes it's difficult to even know how to pray. So here are a few suggestions for how to pray for those going through tragedy, grief, and loss.

First, pray that God's spirit will surround them and strengthen them. Unfortunately, countless things must be taken care of in the days following a tragedy or unexpected loss, and some things won't wait. It is important that people can draw on supernatural strength in these times because if we relied on our own strength, we probably would come up short. Too often, our human response resembles curling up in a ball in our bed and trying to avoid reality. When we feel like giving up, we need God's strength to face each day with resolve to get through it. I'm so thankful that "God is our refuge and strength, a very present help in trouble" (Ps. 46:1).

Second, pray for peace and comfort. Maybe we cannot be with someone to offer personal comfort, but we can pray that others will come alongside with a strong arm to lean on or a tangible way to bring comfort.

Third, pray for healing. Those who experience tragedy suffer emotionally, physically, and mentally—in a manner beyond our comprehension. Often the wounds are hidden under the surface and take years to heal. Don't expect a quick fix. Instead, plan to be the one that continues to encourage and pray for them as they move to a place of healing.

Fourth, pray for hope. Loss of hope is one of the most common effects of tragedy. Often, fear triumphs, and hope turns to despair. It is important, at some point, to lift our eyes off our own troubles and fix our eyes on Jesus if we want to be victorious. For those going through grief, we need to pray they will be strong and take heart and find hope in the Lord (Ps. 31:24).

Fifth, if you are not able to physically meet with them for prayer, pray they will find a friend who can share their burden and pray with them. When we talk to a like-minded believer and ask this friend to pray with us, we feel the burden is lighter because someone is helping us carry it. Great comfort comes from having friends who understand the wisdom of prayer and who can stand beside us when we are going through difficult times. This is especially true of those who are dealing with great loss. They need a friend they can lean on, one who will listen and empathize.

We also should remember that the need for prayer does not stop when the crisis appears to be over. Instead, people who have experienced a life-changing event have a long road ahead. They will need prayer for weeks, months, and even years as they endeavor to navigate the winding path of life in the coming days.

Reflecting on Your Journey

Did you go through a period where you found it hard to pray?

What was the key to finding connection with God again?

How are you doing at praying for others?

10

IT'S NOT A SIGN OF WEAKNESS

Grief is not a disorder, a disease, or a sign of weakness. It is an emotional, physical and spiritual necessity, the price you pay for love. The only cure for grief is to grieve.
—Earl Grollman

Immediately following Janette's funeral, the chaplain invited us to attend a weekly grief support group at the funeral home. It wasn't convenient for us, since we were already planning to travel extensively, so we didn't join. At the time, I didn't think I needed it, and I wasn't sure I *wanted* to share my innermost feelings with strangers. *What would I say without sobbing?* We courteously declined the offer and forgot about it.

Some people imply that support groups are a sign of weakness and that true strength is hiding our grief or pretending it doesn't exist. I disagree, even though I didn't participate in the support group.

Maybe the people who participate in a group are stronger than I am—you know, the one who didn't want to be vulnerable with strangers! It takes a certain type of strength to reach out and receive help when you are going through a deep, difficult time. So, never let anyone suggest that you are weak if you seek help in dealing with your grief. I think true strength is demonstrated by grieving deeply and fully. If you need help, find whatever form of help suits your personality and your journey. Maybe it is joining a support group, confiding in a close friend, or seeking out a Christian counselor. Do whatever feels right to you. My support came in a completely different way that made sense for me.

We received a special package while we were at our camp meeting and mission headquarters in Florida. It was mailed to us by Tom Sproles. We barely knew him at the time, but since then, he has become a special friend. Tom heard about our tragedy and took the initiative to send us several books dealing with grief. It is no wonder that Tom has become a top-notch funeral director who gives excellent, caring service to grieving families in their time of loss.

I don't even remember the titles of the books he sent, and we will probably never know the true value and benefit of those books. But I am certain they made a significant impact on our process of healing.

I began reading them as soon as we returned to my parents' home in Canada where we spent the next several weeks preparing for our missionary fund-raising tour. Ed was scheduling services with churches and pastors, and I was immersed in the books, trying to learn whatever I could that would help us. I love to study and learn, and this gave me a way to try to make sense of what we were going through.

Grief can make us feel extremely isolated. We suddenly find ourselves thrust into a situation for which we haven't been prepared, and we struggle to know what to do. It's as if we've been thrown overboard into the vast nothingness of the ocean and we don't know how to swim. Gasping for air, we think our situation is unique and that no one else has ever flailed around, just trying to keep their head above water. As I explored the concepts in those books, I was able to identify and understand emotions and reactions in myself as normal. It was deeply comforting to realize I was not alone.

One significant point I learned was the importance of protecting our marriage. Without question, the loss of a child puts strain on a marriage. However, if couples are committed to doing what is necessary, a marriage can survive and even strengthen when hard times come.

In a paper on parental bereavement published in *Journal of Nursing Scholarship* in 2003, the authors take note of four contributing factors to marital stress: gender differences in grieving styles, quality of marriage prior to the child's death, cause and circumstances of death, and displacement of anger and blame onto the spouse. Experts agree that maintaining the ability to tolerate a partner's grieving style, keeping open lines of communication, developing a support system beyond that of one's partner, and making a commitment to remain married despite the stress all contribute to marital survival.[2]

In our early days of pastoral ministry, when our girls were toddlers, Ed and I experienced the dismal side of this phenomenon. A young Christian couple who attended a neighboring church suffered an early morning house fire while the husband was in the barn milking the cows. His wife tried desperately to gather the three young children together and get them out of the house. She managed to get them all to a window, and she proceeded to break the window to help them escape. When she turned to get them out, she couldn't find them. The smoke was overtaking her. After a few moments of intense agony, she finally managed to escape—alone. Within a year, their marriage was over. Perhaps all four of the contributing factors mentioned above played a role in the eventual failure of their relationship, but it didn't lessen the sadness that we felt over their separation. We had hoped they could find comfort in God, forgiveness for each other, and grace to search for hope in their time of deepest distress.

Ed and I have always been intentional about safeguarding our marriage, but we became even more so after Janette's death. It is better to be proactive about protecting what might be under attack rather than trying to fix a relationship after it is broken. Thankfully, our marriage was extremely stable when we were cast into the unknown waters of tragedy and loss. Only a few months prior to Janette's death, Ed and I took a retreat to Switzerland where we managed to get some temporary relief from cultural fatigue and engage in times of transparent communication that strengthened our already strong commitment to our marriage. I believe it helped prepare us for the time of crisis that was ahead and equipped us to overcome the obstacles we would encounter in the coming months.

In my reading, I not only learned the importance of strengthening our marriage, but I also learned how important it is to give others freedom to grieve in their own way. As I said earlier, part of my style of grieving was learning as much as I could so I could make sense out of my situation. I'm a thinker by nature. Ed, on the other hand, is a feeler and didn't see as much importance in understanding the concepts as he did in processing his emotions.

Nevertheless, he did listen as I shared what I learned, and one concept that encouraged him was the analogy of grief to the waves of the sea. In the early stages, the waves come in rapid succession. They are high and deep, and they knock us off our feet. We discovered that over time, we could expect the waves to be further apart and shallower. That gave us hope.

Not only was it important for us to be willing to allow the other to grieve in their own way, but it was also important to realize that Alicia had her own style of grief and would take her own journey. Once again, the books were a great resource that helped me become aware of what to look for in children who lose someone close to them.

Looking back, we all realize that Alicia's grief was partially delayed because of our situation in the months following the funeral. Part of the time, we lived with my parents. For several months after that, we traveled to various churches to represent our ministry, staying with family and friends. Alicia received lots of love, gifts, and attention that she otherwise would not have received. Although she missed Janette, the increased activity and acts of kindness kept her mind off the loss. It wasn't until a year later, when we returned to Ukraine, that she entered what I recognized as the full grieving process. That is when reality seemed to set in for Alicia. She missed the constant companionship of her sister and she started to comprehend the impact of Janette's death.

One of the books I read explained the concept of the stages of grief. The stages were laid out step-by-step, and the author even gave approximate time frames for each stage:

1. Denial
2. Feelings of Anger
3. Act of Bargaining
4. Feelings of Depression
5. Acceptance [3]

I found this information interesting, but unlike what the author described, my grief did not fit precisely into these stages. My experience seemed more like a game of Scrabble that was dumped on the floor with all the words and stages mixed up together. I would say these elements all existed in my grief from the beginning, and some came to the forefront at various points, but not in this order and never just for a certain season. It was more of a cyclical process, like the scrambler ride at an amusement park. I think personality can also contribute to a person's journey, and these stages reflect the author's research, no doubt. But I hardly remember experiencing the first three stages. Instead, I spent a lot of time jumping between stages four and five. Nevertheless, it was good for me to understand these stages so I could recognize them in others as a normal part of the grieving process.

Regardless of how you work through and understand the grief you are experiencing, the important thing to remember is that it is not a sign of weakness to seek help. Asking for what you need is a sign of strength. What is ultimately important is that each of us must find a way to work through the negative thoughts, behaviors, and emotions that accompany grief. Grieving is necessary, but there isn't a uniform, cookie-cutter approach to overcoming grief that works for everyone. We are unique individuals, and each of us must find the tools and resources that work best for us. Of course, everyone can benefit from diving deep into God's Word, listening to uplifting music, and believing in a future dream. Other parts of the journey may look distinctively different for each person, so embrace your journey and give ample grace to others whose journey looks different than yours.

Reflecting on Your Journey

Were you ever fearful that seeking help to deal with grief was a sign of weakness?

What actions did you take that helped you to be victorious as you worked through your grief?

What do you wish you had done differently?

11

DRIVING IN THE FOG

I know in my head that she has gone. The only difference is that I am getting used to the pain. It's like discovering a great hole in the ground. To begin with, you forget it's there and keep falling in. After a while, it's still there, but you learn to walk around it.
—Rachel Joyce

All too soon the day came to set out on our support-raising tour. It was vital that we visit churches to represent our ministry and give them the opportunity to partner with us.

Looking back, I wonder, *What were we thinking?* We traveled thousands of miles and spoke three or four times per week for five months, each time in a new location. Most of the time, we were ticking off the miles in our Ford van, crisscrossing the United States. But we also flew to Alaska to visit supporters there. The schedule was grueling, but the family of God was incredibly kind and supportive, and that made it possible for us to keep going.

In each service, I shared a brief account of the accident. We felt it was important to convey the facts to our friends and supporters and let them know that our commitment to the mission had not changed because of our tragedy. Often people wonder if it is okay to talk to someone about their loved one who has passed away, so we wanted to be sure to let people know we were not burying the pain and it was fine to talk about Janette and ask questions. The simple retelling of the story helped clear the air and make everyone more comfortable. Was it hard? Yes. But it was the right thing to do, and I believe it also brought healing.

After a service one Sunday evening, we needed to travel to our accommodations over a mountain in Pennsylvania. As we wound along the twisting mountain road, we became enveloped in a deep, dense, blinding fog. Terror clenched my chest as I peered out the windshield and in futility tried to see the road. I was paralyzed by fear. I was certain we were going to plunge off one of those hairpin turns and roll to the bottom of the mountain. Stopping wasn't an option. If another car came up behind us while we were stopped, they would undoubtedly crash into us because of zero visibility.

We kept going because there was nowhere to stop. If ever I prayed without ceasing, for what seemed like an eternity, it was that night. I silently pleaded with God to have mercy on us. Thankfully, Ed is a good driver. But even he admitted there were times he was uncertain where the road was. It was a miracle we made it safely to the foot of the mountain and out of the fog.

According to conventional wisdom, it was time for us to move on from our grief. In her book, *It's OK That You're Not OK,* Megan Devine states, "We have it deeply engrained in us that any kind of hardship shouldn't last more than a couple of months, at most. Anything more than that is considered malingering. As though the loss of someone you love were just a temporary inconvenience, something minor, and surely not something to stay upset over."[4]

Our lives had changed drastically, but it was expected that we should be over it. Unfortunately, I don't think we ever "get over it" or "move on" from our grief. It is like a heavy fog that stays with us as we move. All we can do is move forward with it. Furthermore, we can't stop. Stopping only gets us stuck in a pit of despair that can lead to disastrous consequences. Moving forward is imperative, so we make a conscious effort to rise and live again. Our grief is not left behind. It is not buried. We carry it with us. And just like carrying any burden, carrying our burden of grief makes us stronger.

From time to time, the fog lifts, and we perceive how God has guided us through the most dangerous terrain of our journey.

Moving forward means we must accept the reality of the loss and realize that life will never be the same again. This is particularly difficult if we were incredibly happy prior to the loss. It is as if we are suspended in a fog between a familiar, pleasant past—to which we can never return—and an unknown future that is clouded from our view. We know we can't go back, but the journey into the future seems intimidating, possibly even paralyzing. Where do we get the courage to face the future?

In these moments, it is crucial to avoid self-pity. It is simple for us to allow ourselves to get stuck in the fog because we drown ourselves in self-pity when hardship or tragedy strikes. We need to realize we are not the only ones who have ever endured hardship or a catastrophic loss. Understanding that others have managed to overcome their difficulties can give us the courage and stamina to face our situation with perseverance and determination.

Life also has a way of mandating that we move forward. The world does not stand still because of our tragedy. I think this is a good thing. Children still need to be clothed and fed. The cooking and housework still need to be done. The job still requires that you clock-in each day. Sometimes the need to perform necessary, routine, daily tasks is the catalyst we need to just keep moving forward by living in the present and taking one step at a time. Keep moving forward. Don't stop or back up!

Invariably, we will experience difficult days when we don't feel like we can keep moving forward. To avoid getting stuck in the fog, it is beneficial to draw strength from others.

Ed and I have distinctive personalities, and our differences allowed us to be strong in specific areas and at various times. During the times when I was struggling, he was strong. When he was discouraged, I could see a ray of hope. This meant we managed to keep each other from getting stuck in a dangerous place, and we eventually moved forward together. Maybe you lost your spouse, so you are missing the exact person you need to help you in the darkest times. I would like to encourage you to find someone you can call on when you need motivation to keep moving forward. Make sure it is someone who will be tough enough to speak the truth when you need to hear it.

Somehow, God helped us to use the months following our tragedy to cultivate a strong focus that helped us to keep moving forward, even during the fog.

I would encourage you to do the same. Reflect on your past and think about your future. Ask yourself: *What do I want my future to look like? Do I really want it to be exactly like the past? Do I want to continue to make the same mistakes I have been making? What do I want to accomplish before my short life is over?* Considerable benefit is found in using your pain to carefully examine your life so that you can get a clearer picture of what you want your future to look like, even if it is not the future you previously envisioned.

Perhaps you have wanted to do something for several years but have either lacked the time or just neglected to act on your dreams. The season of life after a loss can be an ideal time to start realizing that dream or ambition.

But a word of caution. Don't use this opportunity to avoid properly dealing with your grief. Avoiding, neglecting, or suppressing grief only prolongs the pain. Following a long-lost dream or ambition can be extremely beneficial if approached correctly, but it can also be damaging if it supplants the natural grieving process. Remember, the only cure for grief is to grieve. Each action should be properly viewed as part of the grieving process—not as a way to replace it with something else.

Another great way to intentionally move forward is to channel energy into a cause you know your loved one cared about. This can make it feel like you are honoring their memory by carrying on the work that was close to their heart. It can bring satisfaction and meaning to what otherwise might be a mundane existence, and it can ultimately bring sunshine to dissipate the fog surrounding you. We did this by offering a student at Kiev Wesley Bible College a scholarship in Janette's name. For several years, we chose a different disadvantaged student to sponsor. We knew Janette would have been thrilled to provide for a student who had a passion for evangelizing their own people, and it brought us comfort to know that her missionary zeal continued to live on.

If we are willing to put forth the effort to move forward, even when we feel like we are in a fog, we can experience the strength that comes from that effort. Just like an athlete exercises to build up physical strength, we build emotional strength and mental resilience by continuing to move forward through our grief. We must accept our new reality; we cannot turn around, and we can't stop. The only option is to move forward.

That said, we do not leave our grief somewhere on the mountain; rather, we carry it with us. Thankfully, the act of moving forward makes it possible for us to get to a place where the fog is less dense. Eventually, the sunshine will break through the fog, and our journey will become more enjoyable again.

Reflecting on Your Journey

Have you felt pressure to move on from your grief?

What have you done to move forward and find a way to bring beauty from ashes?

Have you started to feel the heavy fog lifting?

12

CHOOSING TO FORGIVE

Forgiveness is not forgetting; it is simply denying your pain the right to control your life.
—Corallie Buchannan

We ended our travels around the middle of November. That allowed us to spend Thanksgiving and Christmas with our parents and start making plans for our return to Ukraine. It was a blessing to spend the holidays surrounded by our loved ones. But naturally, we also keenly felt the loss of Janette's presence as we navigated the difficult waters along the strait between joy and sorrow.

I'm sure our parents felt an enormous weight as they watched us, once again, leave the security of our birth countries and return to the country of our calling. By mid-January, our flight touched down in Kiev, and we were ready to resume our ministry in Ukraine.

We returned to our little house, and although it was good to be home, we had to face a barrage of memories as we sorted through Janette's clothing and personal items. Other sights and sounds in Kiev also triggered emotions that often spilled out or had to be controlled by the sheer effort of my will. A Soviet-style truck (they were everywhere) or a snowy day like the day of the accident would flash memories in my mind and cause a wave of sadness to sweep over me.

The one-year anniversary of any tragic death typically sparks a flood of emotions. We awoke on Sunday, February 16, 1997, and prepared to go to church on the other side of the city—as was our custom every Sunday. We felt a keen heaviness as we relived many of the memories from the previous year, but by now we were able to push through and function quite well. When we arrived home from church, Ed let me off at the gate and proceeded to park the mission van before returning to the house for dinner.

When I started to unlock the door, I noticed it was open. One glance inside, and I realized we had been robbed. My heart sank. The house had been ransacked, and a quick glance around confirmed that several items, mainly electronics, were missing. The intruders were obviously looking for money, but thankfully, our cash-hiding system outsmarted them, and they only found about two hundred dollars that was in my travel purse beside our bed.

Because of the political turmoil, the banks in Ukraine were unreliable, and all financial transactions were made in cash. When we came from the United States, we brought cash to last us for several months. We divided it into envelopes, each envelope containing approximately enough money for one month's budget. Consequently, we had several thousand dollars hidden in the house. As I looked around at the chaos of our rooms, I was sure they must have found some of our carefully hidden cash. When I realized they hadn't, relief washed over me and gave me one positive thing to focus on that day.

Now it was time to forgive *again*. This time, the loss was no comparison to losing our precious daughter. But this time we were dealing with a pre-meditated act against us that was not an accident. This process of forgiving was different. We felt violated. Someone intentionally targeted us, and their choice of a day to carry out their crime could not have been worse.

But as the last year had taught me, forgiveness is foundational to a victorious life free from bitterness, anger, and resentment. It is essential if we seek to move beyond our human emotions and feelings. In fact, I believe it is the most important ingredient in successfully navigating the journey of grief. Forgiveness is a conscious decision to surrender our desire to punish the offender. Instead of remaining stalled in unforgiveness, we can experience the liberty that comes from letting go of the expectation of restitution for the wrongs we have suffered.

Forgiving does not mean we pretend it didn't happen. It is not putting on a mask, saying everything is okay, and burying our emotions. This is not a healthy response because it does not take care of the root of the problem. Moving on doesn't mean we have forgiven. If we fail to deal with the root of our problem by trying to suppress it or cover it up, we allow it to ferment and fester, and we set ourselves up for an explosion at some point in the future. This happens when the pressure becomes too much for us to contain. Instead, we need to meet the challenge of forgiving head on with grace and dignity. We need to be willing to do the difficult work of actively offering forgiveness so that we can experience God's peace and power in our lives.

Too often, we cling to unforgiveness because we focus on the injustice we have endured. It is a selfish response that focuses on how we have been violated, and we believe the offender does not deserve our forgiveness. They feel no remorse, so we justify that we, therefore, are entitled to our feelings of unforgiveness.

But we need to guard against investing too much thought and energy into unforgiveness because we will only extend the time needed for healing. Instead of stopping the intense pain we feel, it causes the poison of resentment to spread within us. This prolongs our pain and suffering, and eventually we realize it is robbing us of our happiness. Unforgiveness is usually an internal, personal battle that others cannot see. Instead, all they will notice is the bitterness and malice that permeates our character if we allow it to remain in our heart.

We need to change our focus and realize that forgiving is an act that is undeserved. It is a gift we offer, even when we see no remorse in the other. It is important to do it for ourselves—not just for the person who has caused us harm. Forgiving allows us to leave behind our anger and find joy; to leave behind hatred and find love; to leave behind dysfunction and find stability; and to leave behind judgement and find compassion. We are no longer weighed down by the resentment and hostility that fill an unforgiving heart.

Unforgiveness makes us a prisoner. Before Nelson Mandela left prison, he said, "As I walked out the door toward the gate that would lead to my freedom, I knew if I didn't leave my bitterness and hatred behind, I'd still be in prison."[5] Forgiving is an act of the will; it is not easy. It does not make you weak; it sets you free and makes you strong.

Most of us know we are supposed to forgive, but we do not have the human strength to do it on our own. We face the monumental mountain of forgiveness, and no matter how hard we try to accomplish it in our own strength, we eventually exhaust our human capacity and run out of grace. We must learn to let God be angry for us when we feel violated. This runs against our natural human tendency to want revenge. But if we will make the conscious effort to forgive, we can avoid staying in the prison of unforgiveness.

Forgiving is not forgetting. Perhaps you have heard the teaching that if we forgive fully, we will forget the wrong that was done to us. It is a myth. We are not God, who has a sea of forgetfulness where he throws our sins. (Micah 7:18,19) We are human, which means we cannot forget the wrongs that have been done to us by the sheer force of our will.

People who say, "Just forget it," usually mean, "Bury it and try not to think about it." Unfortunately, burying feelings doesn't work and leads to another whole set of problems that I addressed earlier. Forgiving is remembering with an attitude of submission and a knowledge that we are accessing God's power to be victorious while enduring an unexplained hardship. It is refusing to give your pain the opportunity to control your life. This response will bring peace and contentment to our lives.

I don't know how you have been hurt or violated, but at some point, we will all be required to offer forgiveness to someone who doesn't show any remorse. This perhaps is the most difficult thing we are ever required to do, and it is also the most important grief work we will do. We cannot hold on to past events and allow them to control and define us. If we do this, it gives our painful circumstance more power over us than it deserves.

The trauma itself is not what does the most damage. It's when we allow tragedy to define our lives that the real damage is done. We need to ask God to give us the power to *respond* to our situation—not merely *react* to it. Our response should be to allow God's grace and power to be the bridge that keeps us from plunging into the chasm of self-pity and drowning in the icy waters of bitterness.

Forgiveness is an act of the will. We can choose to be content with our circumstances by expressing our confidence in God's perfect plan, no matter what happens. If we focus on nurturing God's presence in our life, He will provide the power to heal our brokenness and fill our hearts with joy, which leaves less space for anger, grief, and unforgiveness.

Reflecting on Your Journey

Have you found it difficult to forgive? If so, why?

What should you do to get victory in this area?

If you have forgiven freely, thank God for the strength to respond in a spirit of forgiveness.

Strive to maintain an ongoing attitude of forgiveness in your life, even when it is undeserved.

13

THE BIG PICTURE

Choose the life you want and run in that direction. Don't settle for anything else.
—F. E. Marie

The morning of Janette's accident dawned as any other cold winter day in Ukraine. The girls were getting ready to go to school. Always the perfectionist and concerned about her appearance, Janette was stressed out about combing her hair. She was standing in front of the mirror in her bedroom, just off the kitchen, and she was getting more frustrated by the minute. It just wouldn't go right!

Ed was also becoming exasperated. If she didn't hurry up, she would make both girls late for school. Ed was ready to walk out the door to drive them to school and get on with his day. He urged her sharply to just forget about her hair and get her coat on so they could get in the car. His displeasure caused her to burst into tears, and he decided it would be better to give her a few more minutes so she wouldn't have to go to school in what she considered a disheveled mess.

At last, the three of them rushed to the car, and Ed drove to the school as fast and as safely as he could. Ed and Janette were both silent on the way to school, and it was clear the conflict had placed a wedge in their relationship. Ed was still silently seething about how exasperating she could be in her quest to look good. Janette was hurt by the sharp words Ed had spoken and the displeasure she heard in his voice.

They arrived at the school, and the girls got out of the car and headed toward the big, heavy doors on the school building. Before Janette could walk away, Ed stopped her and said, "Hey. Smile. Dad loves you." Those few words totally changed the atmosphere. She immediately flashed a bright smile that brought light to her eyes, and she skipped off into the building. Little did Ed know that by the end of the day there would be no more chances to tell her that he loved her.

Ed has always been so thankful he didn't let her go off to school that morning without patching up their relationship. Yes, he was in a hurry to get on with the important business he had planned for the day. Yet that snapshot in history will forever live on in his mind, and it reminds him of the importance of valuing relationships over accomplishments. It took ten seconds to restore the broken relationship. If he hadn't spoken those few words, he could possibly have lived with regret for the rest of his life. He can't imagine what it would have been like to constantly live with the tormenting thought, *If only I had told her I loved her.*

Regret can put us in a constant state of guilt that limits the healing of our deep emotional wounds. If we let our thoughts dwell on all we wish we had said or done, we keep our wounds open and fresh. Naturally, many of us live with some regrets. We are not perfect. We get too busy and place priority on our accomplishments over our relationships. The pressure of the present causes us to take our eyes off the big picture and what is ultimately important in life.

If we find ourselves in a place where we are living with regrets, we need to find a way to overcome them. We can use loss as an opportunity to take a step back and evaluate our lives so we can avoid making the same mistakes again. Then we can adjust the course of our life to align with our values. We need to ask ourselves, *Where am I headed? What is ultimately most important to me?* It seems that when the waters of life are smooth and without waves, we tend to drift along on the ocean of life. Day after day, we let the daily breezes propel us in any direction. We risk losing clear focus on that point on the horizon where we intend to land.

Obviously, eternity is the most important point on the horizon to keep in view. Heaven is the supreme goal, and we should never lose sight of it. When tragedy struck our lives, it seemed like life stood still. Our plans and activities for that evening and the next day totally changed. Suddenly, those pursuits weren't what mattered anymore. We were living with heaven as the ultimate end-goal of our lives, but now it came barreling to the forefront, and we realized anew how important it was to keep our lives focused in that direction.

It wasn't just about the final goal of our lives, though. We still had goals and desires for our physical existence in the human realm. We were never a family interested in accumulating material stuff, but the tragic loss of life instantly brought our true values into clearer focus. Having more money or earthly possessions became even less important to us from that point on.

Sure, we all have basic human needs. But those are not the things I am talking about here. Our experience made me much more aware of the sharp distinction between *needs* and *wants* and what I would have to trade to be able to acquire those *wants*. I started sifting purchases and goals through a filter: *How much time away from my family would I have to trade to accumulate enough money to buy this thing I don't need? Is the trade-off worth it in the long run? Why do I want this? Am I looking for it to satisfy a spiritual lack that I should be seeking an answer for somewhere else?* Another question I started asking myself is, *Can I get along without it?* It is amazing how much baggage we can throw off by looking at life through a lens that has a clear focus on eternal values.

It became crystal clear to us that faith and family were the biggest priorities for us. I know we all say this, and we even believe it, but when we evaluated our lives, we realized that sometimes we didn't demonstrate our belief through our actions. It is all too easy to let our work or other responsibilities squeeze out our true devotion to God and our commitment to our family. We get so busy doing what is urgent that we let the truly important things slip. A definite challenge for us in this area is that our work is Christian ministry, so it is easy to let the lines get a little blurred, and it is difficult to keep the proper tension between work and faith. If we aren't careful, we can slip into a situation where we think it is okay to let our Christian work come before our personal faith or our dedication to our family.

At the same time, I believe the early loss of Janette's life intensified our commitment to our missionary service. Many people were surprised when we returned to Ukraine and continued our ministry after her death, but we never considered quitting or leaving the country of our calling. Yes, it took stamina and determination to rebuild our lives and continue our missionary service, but we were more convinced than ever of the importance of the Great Commission to take the Gospel to all nations. We were laser focused on eternal values, and that meant making whatever personal sacrifices were necessary to take the Gospel to those who were hungry to hear.

It takes constant effort to avoid letting the philosophy of our society dictate our goals, desires, and the direction of our lives. We are pushed and squeezed at every turn to accept a materialistic worldview that reduces our ability to objectively see life from God's eternal perspective. We need to constantly keep our eyes on the big picture and not allow ourselves to become dragged down by small thinking and insignificant, selfish desires. When we align our daily goals with the important principles of God's Word, we will find contentment and satisfaction beyond comprehension.

Reflecting on Your Journey

How has your grief experience changed or solidified your values?

What do you want to change today so you won't have regrets later?

14

ADJUSTING OUR EXPECTATIONS

When you release expectations, you are free to enjoy things for what they are instead of what you think they should be.
—Mandy Hale

This brings us to the all-important question: What is the key to surviving the long journey of grief? Can we thrive amid recurring waves of grief, disappointment, and remorse?

I certainly do not have all the answers, but my reflective personality means I have spent a considerable amount of time trying to figure out how to climb to the top of the hill and not remain in the valley. It is important to identify what we can do to have a full, productive life after a devastating loss. Taking the necessary steps to get there has not always been easy. At times, I became weary. I even lost my footing and slipped back a bit. But following the path out of the valley has been worth every ounce of effort I have put into it.

Recently, I saw a video of a grand, formidable building being demolished. It was a controlled, single explosion that reduced the stately old building to a pile of rubble. Surprisingly, the adjacent building didn't suffer any damage at all. In many ways, it was distressing to see the magnificent building become unrecognizable in just a few short seconds. In the place it once stood was a large, empty space and a mound of broken pieces of bricks, mortar, cement, wood, and glass. No part of the previously impressive building was recognizable.

Likewise, we have all seen the footage of the Twin Towers collapsing in front of our eyes during the attack on 9/11. Buildings that seem invincible can stand strong and tall one minute and be destroyed the next due to a single traumatic event.

I can't help but see the analogy of demolished buildings to people who experience tragedy. We are shaken, and we crumble under the sheer force of the unexpected blast. One minute, our lives are secure and predictable; the next minute, our lives don't resemble anything familiar to us. We are left stumbling over a pile of the unidentifiable pieces of our shattered existence.

I attended college on a campus where an old building was torn down and a new, modern building was erected in its place. As you enter the new building, you see an impressive wall made from bricks retrieved from the pile of rubble after the old building was demolished. It's not a perfectly smooth wall because the bricks are obviously not put back together as they were in the original building. Some of the bricks are chipped and broken, but somehow a skilled mason was able to create something solid and attractive from the crumbled pieces that were retrieved from the trash heap.

I love that wall. When I look at it, I am reminded that no matter how devastated we are by our tragedy, no matter how chipped and broken we feel, we can take the fragmented pieces of our lives and rebuild something strong and beautiful.

It takes concerted energy and a clear vision to rebuild our lives from a pile of bricks that have fallen in a heap. The task isn't easy. It's more difficult to take broken materials and construct a building than it is to begin with brand new materials delivered from the lumber yard. In the same way, this rebuilding of our lives is an ongoing process of sorting through what is left to decide what we can salvage and what we need to replace. Perhaps the most difficult part of this process is realizing that some parts of our lives will never return to what they were before our tragedy because they are shattered beyond repair. They must be replaced with something new.

Often, these are the parts we treasured the most, and we now realize that life will never be the same. It is imperative to deal with this reality so that we can move forward with a fulfilling life. We cannot allow ourselves to simply lay down on top of the rubble of our collapsed building, or we will never achieve the beauty of a reconstructed life.

A fundamental key when we are seeking to rebuild our lives is the ability to adjust our expectations for the future. Suddenly, the trajectory of our life has veered off the original course, and what we envisioned for our life is now impossible. It's as if we are forced to take a detour on rough, bumpy roads instead of sailing along on the smooth highway. So, we need to adjust our expectations to align them with reality.

Evaluating and adjusting our expectations and putting them in perspective can be a wearisome task, but it is an extremely valuable exercise that is worth the effort. If we are successful in adjusting our expectations, we avoid allowing the hardships and sorrow to crush us or cause us to collapse into bitterness and self-pity.

When we lose a loved one, we don't just lose them at that specific point in time. We lose the dreams of the happy future we envisioned together and their presence in every future point in our lives.

I had expectations of many pleasant years with Janette, sharing daily joys and merry family celebrations. I expected to adjust her veil on her wedding day and be by her side when she gave birth to our grandchildren. I was certain she would succeed at whatever she decided to do, and I looked forward to watching her soar. Her zest for life and zeal for ministry encouraged me to face the future with positive anticipation. She saw opportunities and possibilities, and she tackled every situation with vivacious tenacity. I also had an expectation that she would share her enthusiasm for ministry with us for several more years in Ukraine.

The day of her accident, she told Pavel, our Ukrainian ministry leader, that we had decided to continue serving in Ukraine until she turned sixteen. She was thrilled with the plan because she had fully embraced our overseas life and ministry. Pavel joked with her that he would look for a good Ukrainian guy for her so they could keep her indefinitely. She laughed, and her eyes sparkled. Then, she became silent, and he watched as the wheels in her head started turning.

Suddenly, those dreams for the future exploded and came crashing to the ground. I wondered, W*hat will life look like without her?* Immediately after the loss, it was unimaginable. I didn't believe that life could ever be pleasant again because the pain was too acute. I needed to cry out to God for help as I tried to adjust my expectations to come in line with reality.

It was normal for me to expect that Janette would outlive me. My vision of my future never included life without her. Frankly, no one expects to outlive their children because statistics are in favor of children outliving their parents. This is one reason that losing a child is different than losing a parent. Of course, we grieve the loss of our parents, and we miss them deeply. But we expect to outlive them. When we lose a child, we are shocked that the normal, expected flow of life has been disrupted, and along with it, a mountain of dreams and plans crash on our rubble heap. Coming to terms with this unnatural turn of events can put us on the path to healing.

Alicia expressed to me recently that this has been the most difficult part of her journey. Immediately after Janette's death, Alicia missed having her as a constant companion, someone who kept life interesting because of her creative imagination. Janette's empty bed in their shared bedroom was a constant reminder of what she was missing. She had taken for granted that they would grow up together. As she has grown older, she wishes she could have Janette as an adult friend and someone to confide in. She still sometimes wishes her children had cousins who could become their lifelong friends. Of course, those dreams will never be realized, and expectations must be adjusted to reality. Nevertheless, it is normal to sense the loss of unfulfilled expectations.

Can we see life in the present as good, even if it didn't turn out as we imagined? It is important we don't allow ourselves to give up on the present because we are disappointed that it didn't turn out as we expected. We need to look for beauty and find meaning in our current situation. Our attitude will determine whether we find joy in our re-adjusted life or whether we live a miserable existence focused on the death of our dreams and plans. We need to accept that something different than what we expected can also be beautiful and enjoyable.

We also need to be careful we don't avoid those places and situations that remind us of our pain and our shattered expectations. It is easy to arrange our thoughts and actions in a way that allows us to circumvent the reality of our tragedy. Some people avoid a place that reminds them of their loss, or they bury their thoughts and resist times of contemplation that could help them come to terms with their situation in a positive way.

If we try to forget the past, we will find ourselves stuck in the dark dungeon of denial with no way of escape. Allowing the light of truth to shine on our brokenness will keep us on the path to healing.

It can be difficult to strike the proper balance between fully grieving for the purpose of healing and grieving indefinitely without accepting reality. If we continue to dwell too much on our loss without a focus on rebuilding a satisfying life, we risk punishing those who live on with us. By continuing to view our life through a negative lens, we also rob those around us of experiencing a life of hope, joy, and fulfillment.

When Janette died, we had to shift our focus to concentrate on building a rewarding life with Alicia rather than pining for something that would never exist. It was a commitment Ed and I took seriously.

Some people unsuccessfully attempt to fill the void left by loss with something else. Instead, I decided to embrace the void. In my mind, my life had a hole smashed through one wall when Janette died. Nothing will adequately fill that space because nothing will replace her. So, my rebuilt life has an archway that I have created from that broken wall, and it leads to a beautiful garden filled with flowers and butterflies. It is my garden of memories from those years that Janette graced our lives with her buoyant personality. I didn't seek to fill the void she left with something else. Instead, I chose to allow the beauty of our shared past to continue to permeate those places that were left empty.

As I look back over the years since Janette's death, I am reminded that the ability to adjust our expectations gracefully is a key to surviving the lifelong journey of grief. It isn't something we do once and it is done. Instead, it is a continual adjustment that we make.

All of us will discover the disappointment of unfulfilled expectations at some time in our life. But if we respond appropriately, we will experience the personal victories that put us at peace with God's perfect plan for us.

Reflecting on Your Journey

What expectations have been unfulfilled because of your loss?

Have you learned to embrace the void that is left in your life?

15

FOCUS ON THE POSITIVE

We begin to remember not just that you died but that you lived.
—Unknown

When we were preparing Janette's body for transport from Ukraine to Canada, the caregivers asked me if I had clothes that I wanted to put on her for transport.

I decided to put her in her favorite pale blue sweat suit pajamas with red heart button decorations and white socks. It was winter in Ukraine, and my "mother heart" sought to keep her warm in the iron casket, even though I knew she wasn't feeling the cold. It was a small comfort to think of her wrapped in her cozy pajamas as she slept all the way to Canada.

After our arrival in Canada, the funeral director gave me an envelope. Inside were four red heart buttons. That small gesture held deep meaning for me, not just at the time but in the years afterwards. It was a symbol that she had lived and loved freely and fully, and that death couldn't take the love for her from my heart. Those buttons became a reminder to me of the vibrant eleven years of life and love that we shared.

At first, when the sting of death was fresh, the reminders were filled with unbidden tears and a focus on what we had lost. As time went on, I started to focus on the positive experiences over her short life that had enriched my life. This shift is important if we are going to successfully navigate the long journey of grief. If we continue to focus on what we have lost, we will be destined for a life of bitterness and hopelessness. If we can successfully shift to viewing our situation in a positive way, we protect ourselves from allowing our spirit to die from despair.

Joyce Meyer says, "Being negative only makes a journey more difficult. You may be given a cactus, but you don't have to sit on it."[6] She has an amazing way of speaking strong truth through a word picture that brings a smile to our faces. Dwelling on the unpleasant circumstances in which we find ourselves is like sitting on a cactus. We must constantly make the decision to respond to our circumstances in a positive way so that we can be victorious.

Memories can be a key component to this process. We were very open in our home about our memories surrounding Janette's life. We would often recount how she would react to certain situations or what we thought she would do if she were with us at that moment. When we sat down to supper and saw a bowl of peas, we would immediately laugh about how she despised peas: "It's a good thing there's also meat and potatoes, or Janette would go hungry tonight."

When we saw a person with worn-out shoes or other pressing needs, we would remember the day she came home from church and announced that she was giving her sneakers to a Ukrainian girl whose shoes were falling apart. "Oh, Janette would be figuring out how she could solve this."

On many occasions, we would smile and comment how her creativity brought so much joy to others: "Remember when Janette wrote that play and got all her friends to help her act it out for us?"

In the years following her death, I appreciated those who shared memories of her with me. It was a way to switch my thoughts from a focus on what I had lost to a focus on how I was blessed over those eleven short years.

She had a bubbly spirit.

"Janette Joy Durham was the epitome of her middle name."
—*Erica (Adams) Emery, friend*

"She was an absolute joy to be around and to have in the classroom when I taught the missionary children." —*Debbie Lindahl, missionary*

She was thoughtful and caring.

"I have a special little pencil and marker set she bought me for the last birthday I had with her. She knew I loved it, but it was kind of expensive. She saved up her money to buy it for me because she knew I would really like it. I have kept it all these years because it reminds me how thoughtful and caring she was to me." —*Alicia, sister*

She had a missionary heart.

"The thing that keeps coming to my mind about Janette is the time in Windsor after we knew you were called to go to Ukraine. I was in the bedroom with the children, watching them play. Janette came over to me and told me that she and Alicia had been talking. They decided that they did not just want to go along with their parents, but they wanted to be missionaries, too. They were sure that there was something that they could do for the Lord in Ukraine. That really touched my heart." —*Gwen Wilson, aunt*

She was a leader and teacher.

"The day before she passed away, she had everyone—including Melvin Jr, who was not very happy about it—sitting in chairs in the boys' room teaching them school." —*Sandy Adams, missionary*

She was creative.

"I struggled a lot with reading for the first three or four years of school. So, Janette made me a special bookmark to use in my readers. She drew my reader with a bookmark in it, and on the opposite side she wrote, 'To the best sister in the world.' She used her creativity to build people up and encourage them to succeed." —*Alicia, sister*

She had a strong relationship with God.

"One special memory I have is the missionary trip we all took to Poland for Christmas vacation one year. On Sunday morning, we gathered in the motel and shared devotions together. I cannot remember exactly what she said, but I remember that Janette gave such a precious testimony that day as we were gathered there. It rang true, and you knew that she really loved God and had a heart to do His will." —*Debbie Lindahl, missionary*

"She was spiritually mature and committed to God. At only eleven years old, she would help friends go pray at the altar and encourage me to read my Bible. God did something special when he made her!" —*Alicia, sister*

"Janette inspired me. She was very deep. You could tell that this little girl loved Jesus with all her heart, and she was passionate about sharing her love for Him. I remember one time in church, I was a little stunned when this eleven-year-old girl beside me stood up to testify with tears streaming down her face. She started quoting Psalms 40:2-3: 'He brought me up also out of a horrible pit, out of the miry clay, and set my feet upon a rock, and established my goings. And he hath put a new song in my mouth, even praise unto our God: many shall see it, and fear, and shall trust in the Lord.' It touched my heart to hear her passion as she was thanking God for bringing her up out of a pit, but my ten-year-old brain was also thinking, *What kind of pit are you talking about? You are just a kid!* Little did I know that our few years of friendship would be cut short." —*Erica (Adams) Emery, friend*

She was kind to those who others left behind.

"She was the only girl, who wasn't a woman, who liked me." —*A young missionary boy who she helped with reading*

"What really sticks in my mind was how she would always include me when the others would try to leave me behind. Daniel and Alicia were so close in age, but I was just a little loudmouth trying to tag along. Janette would let me play with her, and that meant a lot to me. She was definitely the leader of the group, too." —*Beth King, cousin*

She was helpful.

"She helped me comb my long, wavy hair when we visited Grandma and Grandpa one summer. Grandma wasn't sure what to do with it, so Janette took pity on me and found a way to get it under control. Janette would tackle anything!" —*Alicia, sister*

She was a loyal friend who made life fun.

"Janette was full of life! She had eyes that sparkled and a smile that melted your heart. She was a princess one minute and would sit with me weaving wildflower crowns for our princess headdress, and the next minute, she was catching frogs and playing 'cowboys and Indians' with the boys. Life with Janette was full of fun adventures and happy giggles. She was the perfect best friend." —*Erica (Adams) Emery, friend*

By reliving memories, we eventually allow them to bring the peace we are seeking. They fill the void that is left after our loved one is gone. I am so thankful we have happy memories that are too beautiful to forget. Those memories gave us comfort as we were healing.

While it is important to remember the happy memories, we need to guard against viewing the one that has passed away through rose-tinted glasses. I think this is particularly important when we lose a child but have other children still living. If we portray to our remaining children that the departed one was perfect, it leaves them believing in their own insecurities. They can become bitter about the unattainable standard they think they must live up to. Even though Janette brought lots of joy to our lives and the lives of others, we knew she wasn't perfect. We never wanted Alicia to believe that because she wasn't like Janette, we loved her any less.

Janette had many wonderful qualities, but we tried to remain matter of fact about how she challenged us as well. She was strong-willed and determined. She sometimes coerced Alicia into complying with her wishes. I mentioned in an earlier chapter how frustrating her perfectionism was to all of us. After her death, we would mention these things if a situation reminded us of it. "Remember how Janette would stress over . . ." Surprisingly, I think we missed her for her faults, too, and it was important to be open about her shortcomings.

At the time of death, it was easy to view our memories through the lens of what we lost. It was hard for us to imagine a life without Janette's bubbly personality. As time went on, we shifted our perception of the past by focusing on how she had blessed the years we had together. It is how we managed to find joy, not pain, in those memories. Do the memories still bring tears to our eyes? Yes. But we know that by consciously remembering our blessings, we can learn to be happy, even in a life without her. It can protect us from allowing grief to turn into depression.

It can be empowering to realize that our decisions determine the direction of our lives. We are not a product of our circumstances; rather, we are a product of our response to our circumstances. Viewing a situation from another perspective can have a transformational impact on our emotional and physical well-being. It can change the direction of our life. If we can see the blessings instead of only the hardships, we will lift our lives to a level of victory over our circumstances. Our determination must burn brighter than the flames that threaten to destroy us.

Many people find comfort in the months and years after a death by creating reminders of the happy days they had together with their loved one. Some people make a quilt from the person's t-shirts or ties. Others have a keepsake the person gave them. I made a shadowbox with some special things to help me remember Janette and our life together. Sometimes pouring our creative energy into a project after death brings healing and some closure to our grief. Each person will find their own way to focus their energy, and if they cooperate with God, they can find healing on this journey of grief.

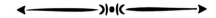

Reflecting on Your Journey

What memories do you have that bring comfort to you?

Have you been able to find a creative way to remember your loved one?

16

EVERYONE'S UNIQUE JOURNEY

It takes strength to make your way through grief, to grab hold of life and let it pull you forward.
—Patti Davis

Recently, I read a story about an elderly Chinese woman who went to a stream every day to get water. She filled two large buckets and carried them back on opposite ends of a long pole she placed across her shoulders. The two buckets were almost identical, except that one had a crack in it and leaked water all the way back to her house. The perfect bucket was full when she arrived back home, but the cracked bucket was only half full.

The cracked bucket felt like a failure because it didn't provide a full bucket of water like the other bucket. So, it spoke to the woman and said, "I am ashamed of myself because this crack in my side causes water to leak out all the way back to your house."

The old woman smiled and said, "Did you notice there are flowers on your side of the path but not on the other bucket's side? I have always known about your flaw, so I planted flower seeds on your side of the path. Every day while we walk back, you water the flowers. For two years, I have been able to pick these beautiful flowers to decorate the table. Without you being just like you are, there would not be this beauty to grace my house and give me so much joy."[7]

This story reminds me that each of us has a unique journey of grief. We shouldn't compare ourselves to others who grieve differently. Maybe we shed more tears or take longer to come to terms with the change in our situation. We need to learn to accept our own personal journey and try to see the beauty in what God is bringing from it. We also need to accept others and realize that their grief is different than ours.

We had to constantly learn this lesson after Janette's death. Ed and I grieved very differently, and it was important to try to understand each other. We would feel the waves of emotion at different times, and the ways we dealt with our emotions were not alike. Keeping communication open was a key to supporting each other in our diverse journeys.

One thing I noticed in the months following Janette's death was that Ed became frantic if he lost something. We all misplace keys or wallets from time to time, but we look and usually find them. Ed, however, went into panic mode when he misplaced something. At first, this frustrated me, and neither of us realized why it was happening. Finally, I figured out it was a reaction to losing something of utmost value that was impossible to replace. When I started to understand why he reacted so strongly, I was able to help him through those situations. Understanding himself also enabled him to respond to his panic rationally.

Grief will show up in a multitude of ways, even ways we don't expect or even recognize at first. Staying aware and endeavoring to understand our family members will help us survive the twists and turns on the path through grief. And if we are willing to accept ourselves and others exactly how we are, we will recognize the ways God uses our pain to water beautiful flowers along our way.

Although everyone's journey is unique, we can all take specific actions to effectively deal with our grief. Implementing the following practices will help you avoid getting stalled in a dark place where you can't find our way out.

Accept your inability to control your circumstances.

I am a planner. I want everything to fit within my perceived best-case scenario. In the early years of our marriage, I was completely happy with my two beautiful daughters and our perfect family. When tragedy disrupted that plan, I was thrown into circumstances I would have never chosen. This was not my plan, but it was my reality. I needed to learn to accept my situation and my inability to control it. At first, I struggled with accepting that Janette wasn't coming back and that our family would never be the same. But as I came to accept it and embrace it, I found joy again in my current situation and hope for a bright future.

Maybe you have come through a bitter divorce and find the life you expected has crashed around you. You will grieve deeply the loss of the future you anticipated, but at some point, you must also accept that you cannot control your present circumstances. You must adjust or be destroyed. How you respond to your situation will determine whether you are miserable or find joy on your new path.

Be willing to share openly with others.

I mentioned in an earlier chapter how we shared our story with the church congregations in the months following the funeral. I see great benefit in openly sharing your journey with those who are willing to listen. People want to talk about the one they have lost, and we found that it put others at ease when we were open about our experience.

It is important to avoid closing your feelings in because it stifles your healing and alienates you from the compassion others want to express to you. Not everyone will have the opportunity to share as openly and often in the months following their loss as we did with ours. But it is healthy to find at least one person who will listen with compassion as you work through your grief.

Social media is a great resource for sharing and learning from others who are also going through a hard time. You can join a group on grief and interact with others who are also facing loss. Sharing in this format can be especially helpful and therapeutic. You learn that your experience is normal; you become aware of different ways of coping; and you may find that openly giving and receiving soothes your pain and uplifts your life.

Learn how to navigate the difficult questions.

To this day, when I first meet someone, I still struggle a little with the question, "How many children do you have?"

I usually decide how close the relationship with the person will be, and then I choose my response accordingly. If I think it will be a distant relationship or if I'm not ready to be completely open with them, I answer, "One. A beautiful daughter who is married and has three boys." If it is someone who I think will get closer to me and needs to understand my life in its entirety, I will say, "Two daughters. One is married and has three boys; the other went to heaven when she was eleven."

If I don't let some of these people fully understand who I am, they become confused when I speak of a time "when the girls were little" or make other references to the season in our lives when Janette was alive.

Your difficult question will no doubt be different than mine. The first time you encounter the question, you might be taken off-guard. Take a little time to think about how you want to answer so you are prepared the next time you are asked.

Learn to adjust to the unexpected.

Everyone will experience some circumstances that are less than ideal. It's the way we choose to adjust to our circumstances that will determine whether we live a pleasant or unhappy life. Our response will also affect those around us.

My mother suffered a debilitating stroke at the age of seventy-three, and due to medical limitations, she was not given the immediate treatment that would help her body recover from the effects of the stroke. She was paralyzed on her right side and required constant care for the remaining eleven years of her life. It was a devastating blow, and no doubt she bore a considerable amount of grief at the loss of the life she knew and enjoyed. But I never heard her complain.

Dad became her primary caregiver and always attempted to keep things positive. His goal was to make her laugh every day during those eleven years. Although many of his dreams and plans were dashed when she experienced the stroke, he decided to make the very most of their situation. He took her on long drives where they could enjoy scenery and time together. He took her out to eat almost every day and cared tenderly for her, even in the difficult times.

My parents were a good example of how we can adjust to an unexpected loss and still make the best of it. Although death is a greater and more final loss and your journey will be unique, the lesson is the same: find ways to continue to live.

Identify specific emotions and deal with them thoroughly.

Spend time identifying your specific emotions and why you are experiencing them. Maybe you are angry. Why? What is causing you to feel it? Maybe you were abused, and you are angry because the person who abused you never expressed remorse for their actions. Or maybe you are experiencing guilt because you failed to take certain actions to mend a relationship before your loved one passed away. Fear can also grip our hearts as we anticipate a future without our spouse's companionship or without our parent's love and guidance.

Loneliness and depression are likewise common during times of grief. If you can learn to enjoy solitude as a way of getting a better understanding of yourself, you will avoid letting grief control your life.

Writing in a journal can help you work through some of these emotions. Spending time thinking objectively about your situation can help you discover ways to resolve your emotions and make peace with yourself. Deal openly with yourself and your emotions. Forgive those who have wronged you. Avoid continually torturing yourself because you missed opportunities, or a relationship was incomplete at the time of death. Don't bury your emotions. Instead, deal with them consciously and carefully, or they can reappear later—perhaps in ways you least expect and may not recognize.

Explore new experiences.

Sometimes our natural tendency during a time of grief is to retreat into our own world and avoid others. People who have lost a spouse often feel like they don't fit in anymore and avoid situations where they are with other couples.

Try to avoid the tendency to retreat and, instead, explore new interests, hobbies, or volunteer work. Healing will take place when you make the effort to move beyond your safe parameters to interact with others. Expanding and enriching our lives with new experiences can establish a renewed sense of satisfaction and enjoyment. It can help us replace our grief with a sense of fulfillment.

Find comfort and strength in faith.

For some people, especially those not solidly grounded in their faith, grief can shake them at their foundation. Maybe you blame God for what you think is an injustice that you have had to endure. It may become difficult to pray because you are distant from Him and can't understand why He would allow your loss. You find yourself in a dry place spiritually, and you lack the energy to find your way out.

Even if you don't feel like going to church, the effort will eventually pay off. When we go to church, we are reminded of the promise of heaven, which can console us when we are grieving the loss of a loved one. Also, the fellowship and encouragement of other believers lifts our spirits and soothes our ragged emotions. Keeping a connection to your faith will help you get through the inevitable rough patches on the journey of grief.

Learn to laugh again.

We have heard that laughter is the best medicine. When our grief is fresh, we wonder if we will ever smile or laugh again, but gradually, tears are less frequent and intense. You become able to remember without crying. At first, you might feel guilty about feeling happy, but it is important to allow yourself to relax and laugh as often as you can because it releases the tension of the pent-up emotions of grief. Eventually, laughter will once again come naturally, and you will find yourself on your way to healing.

Regardless of where you find yourself along your unique journey of grief, I hope you will be able to act on some of these suggestions for specific practices that I have found helpful. Healing won't happen all at once, and it's not a race! Give yourself and others plenty of time to progress at an individual pace. Find the strength to let life pull you forward, and don't forget to celebrate your victories.

My prayer is that you will use this season to grow and flourish in the warmth of God's love as you rest in His perfect plan for you.

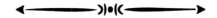

Reflecting on Your Journey

Have you been tempted to compare your journey with that of others?

What area do you need to work on to experience victory on your journey?

17

BROKEN TO SERVE

Blessed be God . . . who comforts us in all our tribulation, that we may be able to comfort them which are in any trouble.
—2 Corinthians 1:3,4

Over the years since Janette's death, Ed and I have had numerous opportunities to share our experiences surrounding the tragedy. Sometimes this took the form of one-on-one interactions with those who were experiencing tragic loss. Other times, we spoke to larger crowds at women's conferences, leadership conferences, church group meetings, and other events around the world.

Just as I was beginning to write this chapter, I was asked to share my story with a group of women in a safe house in Budapest, Hungary, where we currently serve as missionaries. These women are fleeing human trafficking and abuse, and they need a message of hope for surviving the trauma they have experienced. I have found that my trial gives me the empathy to relate to others who are facing pain and loss.

Relating to those who are suffering can be a challenge because they are fragile and vulnerable. Even with the best intentions, we can fail to ease someone's pain and, in fact, deepen it instead. This is the reason we tend to avoid offering comfort to those who are hurting. We are afraid we will say or do the wrong thing.

In an earlier chapter, I mentioned how some of the answers people offered to justify our tragedy were not a comfort to me and didn't provide answers. I have learned that comfort isn't about helping people find answers. We will never comprehend the reasons for some of our pain. Nor is it about finding a solution, though humans have the tendency to want to work out a plan to ease the suffering. Instead, I think comfort comes by acknowledging that the pain the person is going through is real and by encouraging them to trust that there is hope for the future.

Another reason we tend to avoid people who are going through a dark valley is that we are not comfortable with the reality of their agony. Their raw emotions trouble us. We recognize how fragile and vulnerable they are. We feel awkward and helpless. We don't know what to say and are afraid we will say the wrong things. We might even move away from people who are hurting because we are afraid that by getting too close to them, we will end up carrying some of the hurt, too. It is human to try to avoid pain, but sometimes we need to help lift another person's burden by offering sincere comfort.

When I got to this stage in my journey, it was fulfilling to realize there was a redemptive purpose in my pain. Helping others have victory after a time of deep pain and grief brings meaning and satisfaction to us; it reassures us that our suffering was not in vain. I hope you have come to this place in your journey as well. I want to share some tips from lessons I have learned while dealing with my own grief as well as helping others in their time of sorrow. I hope you find these suggestions helpful as you reach out to others who can benefit from your comfort.

Acknowledge that their feelings are legitimate and significant.

Everyone seeks to be understood, so encourage the grieving

person to express their feelings openly. Acknowledge that what they are feeling is valid and normal. Burying emotions only creates deeper problems down the road. Don't try to minimize their emotions or imply that they shouldn't still have certain feelings.

Let them expend their grief on you.

If there is a strong, trusting relationship between you, they may need to share some deep feelings they are experiencing in their current wave of grief. Allow them to unload these emotions on you. This will help them process what they are going through.

Validate their sorrow and offer genuine, heartfelt sympathy.

One way to do this is to simply say, "I know you are hurting. I am so sorry you are going through this." Another way is to offer to pray with them.

Try to discern their mood and respond accordingly.

If they are happy; laugh with them. If they are sad; cry with them. Allow them to experience a whole range of emotions as this will contribute to their emotional, spiritual, and even physical healing.

Make every effort possible to comprehend the depth of their suffering.

Endeavor to communicate this to them through your actions. Allow them to be weak. Don't expect them to be strong. Strength will eventually come, but it is something that is developed over time.

Be comfortable with silence.

Sometimes your quiet presence is more comforting than your words. Offering a hug or holding their hand demonstrates your concern and care.

Listen more than you speak.

Don't assume you know what they are feeling. Let them tell you.

Often a listening ear will give them the courage to see how they can move forward. Avoid offering unsolicited advice; let them explore their own answers to their questions.

Let them talk about their loved one.

Grieving people want to remember the one they have lost, and they want you to remember them, too. Initiate sharing a memory about their loved one. Show them that you are comfortable talking about their memories and you haven't forgotten them.

Focus on them and their situation.

Sometimes it is fine to share your own personal experience to offer hope, but be careful you don't shift the focus away from the one currently going through their own deep pain. And do not give the impression that you have overcome your problems effortlessly.

Give them books they can read and work through as they feel able.

Be sure to make it clear that the books are a gift. You are not lending the books as that creates an extra burden if they need to remember to return them later. They might feel they are taking too long, or they might forget to return them. It takes a lot of pressure off people if they know there is no time limit and they are free to keep these resources.

Point them to scriptures that can bring hope and comfort.

Scriptures like Isaiah 43:2 can be very meaningful during a time of trial: "When you pass through the waters, I will be with you. And when you pass through the rivers, they will not sweep over you. When you walk through the fire, you will not be burned. The flames will not set you ablaze."

Help them realize that moving on doesn't mean forgetting.

Life doesn't stop, and we all must continue to live. Sometimes people feel that if they move on, they are forgetting their loved one.

You can move on with your life and at the same time keep the memory of the one you lost as an important part of you. We grow and change through our grief, but we don't forget.

Encourage them to get professional help, if needed.

If you recognize that a person is continually consumed by grief and the feelings of sadness are not easing, you should encourage them to get professional help. The sadness of losing someone you love never goes away completely, but it should gradually decrease so that it is no longer all-consuming all the time. If someone is stuck in an intense state of grief or with a feeling that life isn't worth living, they may need a professional to help them avoid depression.

Our pain equips us to minister in a more genuine and empathetic way because we understand the deep grief others are going through. We are more likely to recognize their struggles and emotions as normal, and we can often perceive that the pain hasn't gone away even though they appear to be fine.

Over the last couple of years, we have walked with some dear friends through a very deep time of grief. Their long-anticipated baby was born with a congenital disease, and he struggled to live for a short nine months. My heart broke as we stood in the cemetery and watched them bury their dreams and plans in that tiny box on a cool, fall day. We couldn't give answers, but we felt like we understood their heartbreak and confusion. We couldn't solve their grief, but we could offer the promise of God's strength and healing for their deepest wounds.

God has given us the wonderful opportunity to touch many peoples' lives at the crucial time when they needed a word of hope or a comforting touch. Even though we know that hope does not negate the pain, we realize that through telling our story or sitting quietly with those who are grieving, we have encouraged others to find peace in their trials. We still don't know why God allowed our pain and loss, but we know that one of the redemptive purposes of our journey is that we can empathize with others who face tragedy and loss. We don't take lightly the incredible responsibility and privilege we have of being God's hand extended to those who are hurting.

Reflecting on Your Journey

How has God used your experience as a way for you to serve others?

How can you improve in showing empathy to others?

18

DOES TIME HEAL?

Time doesn't heal the wounds; it just helps you process the shock and allows you space to find a new direction . . . Simultaneously, you are building the grief muscles you need to carry the weight of the loss.
—Zoe Clark-Coates

As I mentioned in the introduction, I expected a full and complete recovery within a few months after losing Janette. Now I realize how unrealistic my expectations were. Everyone said, "Time heals." But I discovered that time is relative and probably means for the rest of your life.

The ongoing effects of grief can take all different forms. We successfully deal with one emotion or challenge, and another sweeps over us like a wave. We are constantly adjusting and compensating along the path of grief. It is this resilience that allows us to find peace and victory while traveling through life with our burden.

In the years after the accident, I struggled with the fear of losing Ed or Alicia to another tragedy. I tried to hide my fear, and I never wanted to be overprotective of Alicia as she grew into adulthood. But the struggle was real.

While we were in Ukraine, Ed went to Kiev each Wednesday night for Bible Study. I stayed with Alicia in our house outside the city. If he was late getting home, I became deeply worried something terrible had happened. He didn't have a way to contact me, so I just waited and prayed. It was especially intense during winter months because he drove on treacherous, icy, snow-covered country roads in deep winter darkness on his way home.

Many times, I was sure he had been in a terrible accident, and the torment ripped at my mind and heart. I can remember laying perfectly still in my bed after Alicia had gone to sleep, listening for the sound of him approaching the house. The relief I felt when he pulled in the driveway is difficult to describe.

Over the years, this fear has continued to rear its ugly head at unexpected times. Even after I began writing this book, I realized how Janette's death has affected me deeply and irreparably. The day I finished writing the first chapter, Ed told me he was going out in the evening to help a friend move a piece of furniture with our van. He left at about seven o'clock, and he thought he would be back around nine. He knows how fearful I can be and tries to keep me informed about where he will be and how everything is going. At about ten, he called and said it was taking longer than he expected and that he probably would be home around midnight. I said that was fine, and I settled in for some quiet time.

He wasn't home by twelve-thirty, so I tried to call him on his cell phone. No answer. I started to wonder what had happened to him and called him about every seven minutes; the wait between calls seemed like an eternity. At about one o'clock, I tried to call the friend he was helping, and he also didn't answer. I became frantic. I needed someone to talk to, so I called Alicia in the United States and asked her to pray. She understands the fear I experience when Ed doesn't come home when expected. Darren, my nine-year-old grandson tried to console me: "Don't worry, Grandma. Grandpa probably just lost track of time."

Alone and worried, I grew convinced Ed was in deep danger or dead. I feared he had fallen asleep driving home and had been in a terrible accident. I heard sirens. Probably the ambulance rushing him to the hospital. The only other thing I could imagine was that someone had assaulted him and taken the van keys. He was no doubt lying on the sidewalk, unconscious and unable to call me. Otherwise, I was sure he would call.

Unfortunately, I didn't know the address of the place where he was delivering the furniture, so I couldn't even ask someone to help me go and look for him. At two-thirty, he finally called me and apologized that he had left his phone in the van while in the friend's house setting up the furniture. He lost track of time and thought it was only around twelve-thirty. His friend joked with him that he might be sleeping on the couch.

Was I angry? No. Only incredibly relieved that he was safe.

I don't think I will ever be able to go through something like this without fear involuntarily taking over my emotions. The tragic experiences surrounding Janette's death seem to still dictate my response.

"Unfortunately, research suggests the psychological damage that was done by a child's death often does not heal over time. One study found that even 18 years after losing a child, bereaved parents reported more depressive symptoms, poorer well-being, and more health problems. They were also more likely to have experienced a depressive episode and marital disruption. While some parents did improve, recovery from grief was unrelated to the amount of time since the death."[8]

Before I started writing this book, I wanted to find out if the loss of a child is different than other losses that trigger classic grief responses. In my own experience, I realized that the grief I experienced after my parents' deaths was different than the grief I experienced after Janette's death. Most people who have studied the psychological and biological effects to parents who have lost young children agree that "the trauma is often more intense, the memories and hopes harder to let go of, the mourning process is longer and the potential for recurring or near-constant trauma is far greater than any other type of loss."[9]

I would never diminish the reality of anyone's grief. Every loss or tragedy is very real and painful for those who experience it. However, if you have lost a child, you need to realize that it is a type of grief unlike any other. If the death was a sudden tragedy, it will be even more difficult for you to overcome the ongoing psychological repercussions that you will no doubt have to work through.

Another question I wanted an answer to was, "What about miscarriages and stillbirths?" Many couples are quite open now about the grief they experience when they lose a baby prior to birth. The grief is real, and the parents often go through the normal stages of grief just like any other death. When asked if the grief experienced by parents who miscarry is as devastating as the death of a child who has been alive for many years, Deborah Carr, chair of the Sociology Department at Boston University states, "Not to diminish this experience, but I think not."[10]

Once a child is born, you bond and have life experiences together, so the pain of loss becomes sharper.

Even older adults who outlive their children generally have an easier time coping than parents who lose younger children. "The age of the child is really important because it speaks to promise," Carr says. "When a young child dies, that promise dies with them: the graduation, the marriage, the grandbabies—that's lost too."[11]

This is the reason why holidays and special times of celebration can trigger another new wave of grief. Days that are supposed to be happy times remind us of the person who is missing. Birthdays, Christmas, Mother's Day, Father's Day, and other important dates are bittersweet sometimes for many years after the death. Weddings, graduations, and the birth of children represent the passage of time in peoples' lives and highlight to us that time stopped for our child, and we will never experience these joyous occasions with them.

Although all of this sounds gloomy and depressing, I would like to encourage you, as I have tried throughout this book, to trust that there is power to overcome through God's strength. Yes, at times, the path is steep and rugged, but a few key actions can get us well on our way to healing and thriving, despite our circumstances.

Trust God fully.

If we fail to trust God in all things, we will be miserable, and we will stall on our way to victory. On the other hand, trust releases our will into His hands and brings peace. No matter the difficult situations you face, you will find contentment if you relax and trust God's plan for your life. This is invaluable: "Godliness, with contentment, is great gain" (I Tim. 6:6).

Seek His comfort.

No one can comfort us like God Himself. Our family and friends are an important ingredient in bringing comfort to us at the time of our tragedy, but along the journey for years after, it is important to find comfort in God. He is always available for us to pour out our hearts to Him, and He understands our cries.

Understand yourself.

If we fail to understand ourselves, we will be tormented by our emotions and reactions. If necessary, seek professional help or look for books by Christian authors that will give you good insight and perspective on what you are going through.

Release your expectations.

Realize that life is not a straight line with no hardships from start to finish. It is normal to experience difficulties, loss, and pain. Each traumatic event brings a need for readjusting our expectations based on the emotional and psychological effects of painful experiences. Learn to be satisfied, even if things don't turn out the way you hoped.

Forgive freely.

If someone has wronged you, seek to find forgiveness in your heart, even if they don't ask for it. This is about your victory. It is not about someone paying for their actions that caused your grief. The refusal to forgive will stop your spiritual growth and result in bitterness. Victory is ours if we forgive and refuse to blame others.

Find joy in the present.

The past cannot be changed. Our response to it is a daily decision that will determine the level of our victory. If we are consumed by the tragedy, we will find our lives shattered beyond repair. Instead of dwelling on the past, it is critical to look for joy in the present.

Over the years since Janette's death, God has been very gracious to us, and we have found plenty of reasons to rejoice. He has blessed us with over twenty-five years of fulfilling ministry, and we have thrived as we have followed Him day by day. Alicia married a wonderful Christian man, and she has blossomed into a beautiful wife and mother who loves God. She is a woman of strength and honor who makes us proud. And we have three young grandsons who continue to bring joy to our hearts year after year. Don't wait for things to get better. Life will always have its tests and trials. Learn to be happy right now; otherwise, you will run out of time.

The healing we ultimately experience can be compared to a physical injury. Over time, our bodies have an amazing ability to recover from physical trauma and injury. Lacerations, broken bones, and even incisions from surgery will eventually heal. However, if the injury is significant, tender scars or painful joints continue to remind us of our injury for the rest of our life. People who see me now probably can't see the large, tender scar on my heart. They don't know how my grief has changed me. But I know. And I choose to let it make me stronger and, at the same time, more sensitive to others.

A few years ago, I was introduced to Kintsugi, the Japanese art of putting broken pottery pieces back together with gold. I believe it illustrates how time heals. Kintsugi embraces flaws and imperfections to create an even stronger, more beautiful piece of art. I couldn't help but see the similarities to a life that is shattered by tragedy. We will never be the same; we will always have scars. However, we can allow God to work in our lives, heal our pain, and put the broken pieces back together with seams of gold.

I continue to pray that God will fashion my imperfect vessel into one that is pleasing to Him: strong and beautiful in the places I have been broken, valuable in His service, and demonstrating His power, which gives victory on this journey of grief.

Reflecting on Your Journey

Has your grief lasted longer than you expected?

Have you come to terms with the concept that time doesn't completely heal?

Are you allowing God to put your broken pieces back together with seams of gold?

ENDNOTES

1. https://www.goodreads.com/author/quotes/6264.Elisabeth_Elliot
2. Stephanie Frogge, "The Myth of Divorce Following the Death of a Child," *Taps*, March 1, 2015, https://www.taps.org/articles/21-1/divorce.
3. Elisabeth Kubler Ross, *On Death and Dying* (New York: Macmillan, 1991).
4. Megan Devine, *It's OK That You're Not OK* (Boulder: Sounds True, 2017).
5. https://www.goodreads.com/author/quotes/367338.Nelson_Mandela
6. Joyce Meyer, *Approval Addiction: Overcoming Your Need to Please Everyone* (Brentwood, TN: FaithWords, 2005).
7. https://pollockrandall.com/healing/coping-with-grief/good-things-come-from-leaky-buckets
8. Joshua A. Krisch, "What the Loss of a Child Does to Parents, Psychologically and Biologically," *Fatherly*, June 7, 2021, https://www.fatherly.com/health-science/how-parents-experience-the-death-of-a-child.
9. Ibid.
10. Ibid.
11. Ibid.